ANALYZING THE ISSUES

CRITICAL PERSPECTIVES ON
THE VIABILITY OF
HUMAN LIFE ON
OTHER PLANETS

Edited by Nicki Peter Petrikowski

Enslow Publishing
101 W. 23rd Street
Suite 240
New York, NY 10011
USA

enslow.com

Published in 2017 by Enslow Publishing, LLC
101 W. 23rd Street, Suite 240, New York, NY 10011

Library of Congress Cataloging-in-Publication Data

Names: Petrikowski, Nicki Peter, editor.
Title: Critical perspectives on the viability of human life on other planets
 / edited by Nicki Peter Petrikowski.
Description: New York, NY : Enslow Publishing, 2017. | "2017 | Series:
 Analyzing the issues | Includes bibliographical references and index.
Identifiers: LCCN 2016005255 | ISBN 9780766076747 (library bound)
Subjects: LCSH: Space colonies—Juvenile literature. | Space
 environment—Juvenile literature. | Habitable planets—Juvenile
 literature. | Outer space—Exploration—Juvenile literature.
Classification: LCC TL795.7 .C75 2017 | DDC 629.44/2—dc23
LC record available at http://lccn.loc.gov/2016005255

Printed in the United States of America

To Our Readers: We have done our best to make sure all website addresses
in this book were active and appropriate when we went to press. However,
the author and the publisher have no control over and assume no
liability for the material available on those websites or on any websites
they may link to. Any comments or suggestions can be sent by e-mail to
customerservice@enslow.com.

Excerpts and articles have been reproduced with the permission of the
copyright holders.

Photo Credits: Cover, MICKE Sebastien/Paris Match Archive/Getty Images
(simulation of Mars), Thaiview/Shutterstock.com (background, pp. 4–5
background), gbreezy/Shutterstock.com (magnifying glass on spine); p.
4 Ghornstern/Shutterstock.com (header design element, chapter start
background throughout book).

CONTENTS

INTRODUCTION

Earth will not be able to support human life forever. Eventually, the Sun will expand into a red giant that will engulf the inner planets of our solar system, and possibly Earth as well. Whether our home planet is swallowed by the Sun or not, the heat from our expanding Sun would make life as we know it impossible. One can find solace in the fact that this inevitable fate is more than seven billion years away, so it is not something those who are alive today have to be particularly worried about. Once it is established that Earth has an expiration date, though, the question arises if the human race can find a way to survive beyond its home planet.

Seven billion years, of course, is a very long time for humankind to figure out a way to find a new home. But there are potential dangers that could threaten human life on Earth a lot sooner. The impact of a meteor like the one believed to have played a part in the extinction of the dinosaurs sixty-five million years ago would have catastrophic consequences. The eruption of a supervolcano and the resulting volcanic winter could also lead to human extinction. Infectious diseases could result in a worldwide pandemic. However, the biggest threat to humans is probably the human race itself. Every year we exhaust more natural resources than Earth can regenerate and, with the population constantly growing, this is unlikely to stop. While this in itself is a danger, it also increases the likelihood of war for the remaining resources, which could make Earth uninhabitable. Humanity already stood on the brink of destruction in a nuclear war once, and this danger still exists today.

While it is certainly frightening to think about, there are numerous ways human life on Earth could come to an end. This is why it is worthwhile, or perhaps even imperative, to think about the possibility of developing colonies in space.

So far, human presence in space has been rather small; a total of twelve people have set foot on the Moon as part of the Apollo missions from 1969 to 1972, and a few hundred individuals have visited one of the space stations humans have put in low Earth orbit. Setting up a settlement on another planet would be—to quote Neil Armstrong, the first man on the Moon—a "giant leap for mankind."

We must analyze many aspects when pondering the viability of human life on other planets: Which astronomical objects are suitable candidates for a human colony? Can they support human life? If not, is it possible to change the conditions there so that they can? Once a colony is established on another planet, what will its relationship with Earth be? Who will benefit from the resources of this new planet and who will own the land? And, of course, the big question: How do we get there?

The following articles look at these and other issues to provide different perspectives on the viability of human life on other planets.

CHAPTER 1

WHAT THE EXPERTS AND ACADEMICS SAY

W hen someone jokingly wants to express doubt about the alleged expertise of someone else, it is common to ask, "What are you, a rocket scientist?" When the topic is the viability of human life on other planets, however, the answer to that question is frequently "yes." In addition to rocket scientists, experts from other fields also contribute to the ongoing efforts to make the exploration of space possible. And it is a good thing that some of the smartest people humanity has to offer are contributing their brain-power to this effort. Space is a hostile place, and it presents us with great challenges that will have to be overcome if humans are to live on planets other than Earth in the future. Despite these challenges, many experts are hopeful that humans will be able to colonize another planet at some point. Others remain sceptical that we will find a way to travel the immense distance to a planet capable of supporting human life or manage to raise the vast amount of resources necessary to turn a planet that is easier to reach into a habitable environment. Meanwhile, the National Aeronautics and Space Administration (NASA) and other organizations are in the process of preparing manned missions to Mars, which could be the first step toward settling on another planet. If humanity will be able to find new homes among the stars, only time will tell. Either way, watching as we journey farther into space will be fascinating.

"TO MARS, OR, NOT TO MARS?" BY THOMAS D. TAVERNEY, FROM *THE SPACE REVIEW*, AUGUST 19, 2013

"Mars tugs at the human imagination like no other planet. With a force mightier than gravity, it attracts the eye to the shimmering red presence in the clear night sky..." • John Noble Wilford, *Mars Beckons*

Every civilization seeks to achieve greatness and build monuments to be left to subsequent generations as high water marks of their value, demonstrating their essence, and providing a statement that its people were here. These monuments are crafted by the most import-ant minds and shaped and sculpted by the most skilled hands. They are left proudly to their children, children's children, and for some, scores of generations. The desire to build monuments and innovate is a fundamental attribute of human societies. The greats have left us with the pyramids, the Great Wall, the Panama Canal, the steam engine, railroads, skyscrapers, the screw propeller, the automobile, the airplane, and even cave paintings. Each wonder, each innovation, says that its people were here with their hearts, minds and hands. Great achievements advance the human condition and establish markers of important technical advances.

We are no different today. Over nearly sixty years we have broken free of the gravitational bonds that have anchored us to the planet Earth. Our satellites have visited all the planets, as well as asteroids and comets. We've left bootprints on the surface of the Moon. And although we have achieved many exciting innovations since that moment the flag was planted on the Moon over forty years ago, the Apollo landing remains the pinnacle of our achievement.

Now, as a nation and a people, we are confounded by a new question: To Mars, or, not to Mars? This is a not-so-simple query worthy of an intense national debate and soul searching. And for a spacefaring nation, it's one that generates even more questions. Will it be worth it to go to Mars?

The US economy is currently saddled with a huge debt, and many parts of the global economy are faltering. These are tough times. Millions have been driven from the job market and are no longer counted as unemployed by cynical beancounters in the Labor Department. With little relief in sight, skeptics ask, "Shouldn't we respond first to the basic needs of the people, of mothers and fathers, schools, public safety, the environment, before we commit to such an immense venture? Shouldn't we understand how much of our precious national treasure will be drained to fund it? What has been the real value of space adventures to date?"

Genius heroes like Buzz Aldrin respond magnificently to these disheartening theatrics. Back in 2009, he articulated a perfect response in his book *Magnificent Desolation*:

> "It's not the value of the rocks we brought back, or the great poetic statements that will be uttered. Those things aren't remembered. It's that people witnessed that event. We are not going to justify going to Mars by what we bring back."

To many, it seems a bit of madness to dream that someday we could build a colony on Mars. Then again, perhaps not. When I was born it was considered pure science fiction to imagine an astronaut could travel to the Moon, land and safely return. Yet, Buzz Aldrin and Neil Armstrong did just that. They bounced out and about on the surface of our Moon, and captured the imagination of the world. Millions of us watched with great pride and excitement here in the United States.

These were days when I was still trying to decide my future career and education choices. I remember talking to friends and neighbors and listening to scientific cynics who were quite sure and convinced that advanced electronics would not function in space. Some warned that if people foolishly went to space, their blood would boil. At the very least, they were sure that space travelers would become spatially disoriented and die as a result.

Of course, such hissing has confronted innumerable great achievements. It was not too long ago, for example, when the sound barrier also was thought unassailable. But on October 14, 1947, Chuck Yeager wrapped himself into a rocket ship, secured the door with [a] broom handle because of [a] rib he had broken a day before, and then boldly proved the naysayers wrong. And Yeager's achievement was no more daunting or courageous than the exploits of the early great European explorers who sailed across an uncharted ocean. They didn't know what they would find on the other side. New knowledge and opportunities come from the best and brightest boldly reaching to confront grand challenges. We will only grow as a species by taking risks. They provide a measure of the human spirit.

But isn't the idea of colonizing Mars crazy? Perhaps, but it is also true that the conditions on the surface of Mars are much closer to Earth than the surface of any other body in the solar system. The Martian environment is far better than the extremely hot and cold temperatures on Mercury, the furnace-hot surface of Venus, or the cryogenic temperatures of the outer planets and their moons. Humans have already explored natural settings on Earth that match most conditions on Mars. For example, the highest altitude reached by a manned balloon ascent, a record recently set in the recent Red Bull challenge, is nearly 39,000 meters; the pressure at that altitude is about the same as it is on the surface of Mars. And the extremes of cold in the Arctic and Antarctic match all but the most extreme temperatures on Mars. Overall, however, that Mars is not a very friendly place.

In short, colonizing Mars would pose daunting challenges. So attempting colonization should not be attempted as a first step, nor attempted anywhere near the first steps on a new planet. As with the early Moon excursions, we first should go to Mars, orbit it, and return safely to Earth. Once we are confident that can be successfully achieved on a regular basis, the next step should be to send people there, to assess and explore, and bring them back safely. Next, we need to have visitors begin to build sustainable infrastructure on the planet, and return. Only then, when infrastructure is in place, should we even think of colonizing Mars.

But what would be the value, beyond the "wow" factor? In 1961, President Kennedy answered this eternal question when he described the need for a commitment to go to the Moon before the end of the decade. He said:

> "We choose to go to the moon in this decade, and do the other things, not because they are easy, but, because they are hard, because that goal will serve to organize and measure the best of our energies and skills, because the challenge is one that we. Are willing to accept, one we are unwilling to postpone, and one which we intend to win... No single space project in this period will be more impressive to mankind, or more important to the long term exploration of Space, and none will be so difficult or expensive to accomplish... The decision demands a major national commitment of scientific and technical manpower, material, and facilities."

Kennedy's key point is applicable to any Mars venture would be that it would be invaluable to "organize and measure the best of our energies and skills." Seeking to put the same priority on going to Mars as we did to going to the Moon with Apollo—only now performed as a global endeavor—should serve as a motivation and cata-lyst to drive the global technical innovation engine. The technologies developed for a trip to Mars should produce effects comparable to those produced by technologies we developed for going to the Moon.

Another significant value that could be derived from a human Mars mission is that it will demonstrate US international space technology leadership. The US gained leadership values and lessons from the Cold War competition that drove the development of Apollo and, later, the Space Shuttle. These leadership values then evolved as the US and a number of nations constructed and operated the International Space Station. A drive to successfully travel to Mars could reenergize our domestic engineering industries and industrial base. Students and people inspired by a Mars venture could serve to stimu-late engineering and science innovators who [are] essen-tial to economic and technical growth.

A more subtle benefit to be derived from a human mission to Mars is that it may prove to provide a new understanding of who we are. Finding life, or evidence of past life, on another planet will change us in ways that we can't imagine. The picture of the whole Earth taken by a human on the way to the Moon is still today changing who we are: how beautiful and fragile and interconnected our home the Earth is, with no visible borders.

How can one confront the reasonable arguments against going to Mars? As we have discussed, given the challenges faced by our society, many ask: "Why should we spend billions on space when we have so many problems here on Earth?" One can respond to this type of no-win argumentative question with a question: "We do have many pressing problems today on Earth, but how would we face these problems without the knowledge developed by America's space program in the past 50 years?" Information systems, material technologies, and many other developments have enabled the development of a highly interdependent world. Without space technologies, our society would be left to grapple with the concerns of changing climate without NASA-developed weather and earth observation satellites. Our world would not survive without advanced communications based on NASA developments in communications satellites, error-correcting codes and integrated circuits.

The drive to explore embodies [a] very human and important desire for constant improvement and satisfying curiosity as to what is around the corner. It is this very desire for constant improvement and curiosity that drives our very souls to want to go to Mars. Tens of thousands of people, for example, have expressed an interest in applying for Mars One, a one-way journey to Mars, just as people in the past, back to our distant ancestors, journeyed across the globe. We are never happy with the status quo. We have always been looking to do things in a better way or with a new tool, or trapeze or canoe or sail to a new place, or experience a new adventure.

Can we afford to go to Mars? In a sense, the easy answer is no. We simply have too many pressing needs on Earth and in the United States to spend money on such a frivolous venture. And, to be sure, the cost of a human Mars program would be huge. At this point, even a nation such as the United S[t]ates, with its vast resources, will likely find the cost prohibitive. But, much the same could have been said of the venture of going to the Moon.

Therefore, I believe this challenge needs to be a world-wide endeavor.

Given the cost pressures, should we allow private enterprise to lead the way? Most of the truly astounding inventions and innovations of the 19th and 20th centuries were the product of private individuals: the train, steam ship, airplane, telephone, electric lighting, and more. Spaceflight was the one endeavor that was too expensive for the private entrepreneur to conquer. And, in the early years of the Space Era, there was no immediate return on investment. But have times changed? Should private enterprise take the lead and fly to Mars? The bicycle mechanic Wright Brothers beat professor Samuel Langley to achieve the first sustained heavier-than-air powered flight despite President McKinley providing Langley a $50,000 grubstake to achieve the feat. Langley worked on engines and paid no attention to aerodynamics, aircraft design, flight controls, wind tunnel tests, and the like, all essential to successful flight. The Langley gadget flopped off the house boat into the river time and again. The Wrights did it right and achieve their initial fame without government funding.

One alternative to government-run Mars expeditions may be "Act of Will" organizations. Act of Will entities do not pursue a market to make money as a private company would, they pursue challenges to advance the human accomplishment. Currently there are multiple Act of Will entities involved in the pursuit of going to Mars. Three of the highest profile are Inspiration Mars, which is proceeding with plans to mount a 2018 crewed flyby mission; Golden Spike, investigating mounting a two-person missions to the Moon for brief, Apollo-like stays; and Mars One, which plans to land humans on Mars—to stay—as early as 2023.

Private "Act of Will" entities such as these might be willing, for example, to risk propelling a mission to Mars with innovative technologies to shorten the travel time. They could achieve success with a round trip of reasonably short duration. This would greatly reduce the radiation exposure for astronauts, improving safety. Act of Will entities are also willing to risk loss of a crew, just the way barnstormers and test pilots used to risk their lives. These organizations might also take other risks NASA would never allow. I suspect part of this view is that every year adventure tourists are killed attempting to climb Mount Everest, and yet demand continues to increase.

A substantial fraction of robotic Mars missions have been unsuccessful. Entry, Descent, and Landing (EDL) is complicated and not well understood. Even the best of the best, JPL, has paid precious dollars and put many people to work, testing and retesting every line of code in every sequence possible to make sure the hardware did what it was told to do, autonomously, but has still suffered mission failures.

A trip to Mars and back cannot be easily performed. There will be plenty for private companies to help achieve the feat, however, and there should be critical roles for international partnerships on the grand adventure. Unfortunately, some private entities believe they can simply contract out parts and software, with their only job to assemble mature technologies. They are too optimistic. While these organizations are supported by brilliant engineers, they have not been forged in the crucible of actually getting systems to Mars, as the brilliant engineers at JPL have, and therefore these organizations lack:

- Critical systems engineering skills and experience;
- EDL expertise;
- Focused management teams and program managers responsible for systems engineering, development, integration, and test; and
- Appreciation for the amount of software needed, and development and testing required.

A human Mars mission should be a national goal, stimulated by a grand challenge and significant federal funding. NASA's budget today is roughly half a percent of the federal budget. Doubling that would be lost in the round off error in this overall budget. Going to Mars certainly fits Kennedy's "reaching for new heights" language. While we figure out how to fix the economy, we should also start a conversation about going to Mars as a global endeavor. NASA needs to get some seed money to start defining the difficult problems, and begin developing solutions to some of the key challenges facing human Mars missions. Also, JPL needs to continue to break ground in understanding Mars and the engineering of getting there.

There is no shortage of innovation in this era, and many achievements could be hailed as our greatest contribution to the evolution of the species, from nanotechnology and nuclear energy to genetics and smartphones. Space must compete with other technology pursuits such as sustainable energy, artificial intelligence, and genetic engineering. Is the US ready to step up to a JFK-like challenge once again in space to do, not what is easy, but what is hard?

1. What is the value of traveling to another planet, especially considering the problems we now face on Earth?

EXCERPT FROM "WILL WE EVER COLONIZE MARS?" BY MATT WILLIAMS, FROM *UNIVERSE TODAY*, MAY 31, 2015

Mars. It's a pretty unforgiving place. On this dry, dessicated world, the average surface temperature is -55 °C (-67 °F). And at the poles, temperatures can reach as low as -153 °C (243 °F). Much of that has to do with its thin atmosphere, which is too thin to retain heat (not to mention breathe). So why then is the idea of colonizing Mars so intriguing to us?

Well, there are a number of reasons, which include the similarities between our two planets, the availability of water, the prospects for generating food, oxygen, and building materials on-site. And there's even the long-term benefits of using Mars as a source of raw materials and terraforming it into a liveable environment. Let's go over them one by one…

BENEFITS:

As already mentioned, there are many interesting similarities between Earth and Mars that make it a viable option for colonization. For starters, Mars and Earth have very similar lengths of days. A Martian day is 24 hours and 39 minutes, which means that plants and animals – not to mention human colonists – would find that familiar.

Mars also has an axial tilt that is very similar to Earth's, which means it has the same basic seasonal patterns as our planet (albeit for longer periods of time). Basically, when one hemisphere is pointed towards the Sun, it experiences summer while the other experiences winter – complete with warmer temperatures and longer days.

This too would work well when it comes to growing seasons and would provide colonists with a comforting sense of familiarity and a way of measuring out the year. Much like farmers here on Earth, native Martians would experience a "growing season", a "harvest", and would be able to hold annual festivities to mark the changing of the seasons.

Also, much like Earth, Mars exists within our Sun's habitable zone (aka. "goldilocks zone"), though it is slightly towards its outer edge. Venus is similarly located within this zone, but its location on the inner edge (combined with its thick atmosphere) has led to it becoming the hottest planet in the Solar System. That, combined with its sulfuric acid rains makes Mars a much more attractive option.

Additionally, Mars is closer to Earth than the other Solar planets – except for Venus, but we already covered why it's not a very good option! This would make the process of colonizing it easier. In fact, every few years when the Earth and Mars are at opposition – i.e. when they are closest to each other – the distance varies, making certain "launch windows" ideal for sending colonists.

For example, on April 8th, 2014, Earth and Mars were 92.4 million km (57.4 million miles) apart at opposition. On May 22nd, 2016, they will be 75.3 million km (46.8 million miles) apart, and by July 27th of 2018, a meager 57.6 million km (35.8 million miles) will separate our two worlds. During these windows, getting to Mars would be a matter of months rather than years.

Also, Mars has vast reserves of water in the form of ice. Most of this water ice is located in the polar regions, but surveys of Martian meteorites have suggested that much of it may also be locked away beneath the surface. This water could be extracted and purified for human consumption easily enough.

In his book, *The Case for Mars*, Robert Zubrin also explains how future human colonists might be able to live off the land when traveling to Mars, and eventually colonize it. Instead of bringing all their supplies from Earth – like the inhabitants of the International Space Station – future colonists would be able to make their own air, water, and even fuel by splitting Martian water into oxygen and hydrogen.

Preliminary experiments have shown that Mars soil could be baked into bricks to create protective structures, which would cut down on the amount of materials needed to be shipped to the surface. Earth plants could eventually be grown in Martian soil too, assuming they get enough sunlight and carbon dioxide. Over time, planting on the native soil could also help to create a breathable atmosphere.

CHALLENGES:

Despite the aforementioned benefits, there are also some rather monumental challenges to colonizing the Red Planet. For starters, there is the matter of the average surface temperature, which is anything but hospitable. While temperatures around the equator at midday can reach a balmy 20 °C, at the Curiosity site – the Gale Crater, which is close to the equator – typical nighttime temperatures are as low as -70 °C.

The gravity on Mars is also only about 40% of what we experience on Earth's, which would make adjusting to it quite difficult. According to a NASA report, the effects of zero-gravity on the human body are quite profound, with a loss of up to 5% muscle mass a week and 1% of bone density a month.

Naturally, these losses would be lower on the surface of Mars, where there is at least some gravity. But permanent settlers would still have to contend with the problems of muscle degeneration and osteoporosis in the long run.

And then there's the atmosphere, which is unbreathable. About 95% of the planet's atmosphere is carbon dioxide, which means that in addition to producing breathable air for their habitats, settlers would also not be able to go outside without a pressure suit and bottled oxygen.

Mars also has no global magnetic field comparable to Earth's geomagnetic field. Combined with a thin atmosphere, this means that a significant amount of ionizing radiation is able to reach the Martian surface.

Thanks to measurements taken by the Mars Odyssey spacecraft's Mars Radiation Environment Experiment (MARIE), scientists learned that radiation levels in orbit above Mars are 2.5 times higher than at the International Space Station. Levels on the surface would be lower, but would still be higher than human beings are accustomed to.

In fact, a recent paper submitted by a group of MIT researchers – which analyzed the Mars One plan to colonize the planet beginning in 2020 – concluded that the first astronaut would suffocate after 68 days, while the others would die from a combination of starvation, dehydration, or incineration in an oxygen-rich atmosphere.

In short, the challenges to creating a permanent settlement on Mars are numerous, but not necessarily insurmountable.

TERRAFORMING:

Over time, many or all of the difficulties in living on Mars could be overcome through the application of geoengineering (aka. terraforming). Using organisms like cyanobacteria and phytoplankton, colonists could gradually convert much of the CO_2 in the atmosphere into breathable oxygen.

In addition, it is estimated that there is a significant amount of carbon dioxide (CO_2) in the form of dry ice at the Martian south pole, not to mention absorbed by in the planet's regolith (soil) [sic]. If the temperature of the planet were raised, this ice would sublimate into gas and increase atmospheric pressure. Although it would still not be breathable by humans, it would be sufficient enough to eliminate the need for pressure suits.

A possible way of doing this is by deliberately triggering a greenhouse effect on the planet. This could be
done by importing ammonia ice from the atmospheres
of other planets in our Solar System. Because ammonia
(NH_3) is mostly nitrogen by weight, it could also supply the
buffer gas needed for a breathable atmosphere – much as
it does here on Earth.

Similarly, it would be possible to trigger a greenhouse effect by importing hydrocarbons like methane –
which is common in Titan's atmosphere and on its surface.
This methane could be vented into the atmosphere where
it would act to compound the greenhouse effect.

Zubrin and Chris McKay, an astrobiologist with
NASA's Ames Research center, have also suggested
creating facilities on the surface that could pump greenhouse gases into the atmosphere, thus triggering global
warming (much as they do here on Earth).

Other possibilities exist as well, ranging from
orbital mirrors that would heat the surface to deliberately
impacting the surface with comets. But regardless of the
method, possibilities exist for transforming Mars' environment that could make it more suitable for humans in
the long run – many of which we are currently doing right
here on Earth (with less positive results).

Another proposed solution is building habitats
underground. By building a series of tunnels that connect
between subterranean habitats, settlers could forgo the
need for oxygen tanks and pressure suits when they are
away from home.

Additionally, it would provide protection against
radiation exposure. Based on data obtained by the Mars
Reconnaissance Orbiter, it is also speculated that habit-

able environments exist underground, making it an even more attractive option.

PROPOSED MISSIONS:

NASA's proposed manned mission to Mars – which is slated to take place during the 2030s using the Orion Multi-Purpose Crew Vehicle (MPCV) and the Space Launch System (SLS) – is not the only proposal to send humans to the Red Planet. In addition to other federal space agencies, there are also plans by private corporations and non-profits, some of which are far more ambitious than mere exploration.

The European Space Agency (ESA) has long-term plans to send humans, though they have yet to build a manned spacecraft. Roscosmos, the Russian Federal Space Agency, is also planning a manned Mars mission, with simulations (called Mars-500) having been completed in Russia back in 2011. The ESA is currently participating in these simulations as well.

In 2012, a group of Dutch entrepreneurs revealed plans for a crowdfunded campaign to establish a human Mars base, beginning in 2023. Known as MarsOne, the plan calls for a series of one-way missions to establish a permanent and expanding colony on Mars, which would be financed with the help of media participation.

Other details of the MarsOne plan include sending a telecom orbiter by 2018, a rover in 2020, and the base components and its settlers by 2023. The base would be powered by 3,000 square meters of solar panels and the SpaceX Falcon 9 Heavy rocket would be used to launch the hardware. The first crew of 4 astronauts would land on Mars in 2025; then, every two years, a new crew of 4 astronauts would arrive.

On December 2nd, 2014, NASA's Advanced Human Exploration Systems and Operations Mission Director Jason Crusan and Deputy Associate Administrator for Programs James Reuthner announced tentative support for the Boeing "Affordable Mars Mission Design". Currently planned for the 2030s, the mission profile includes plans for radiation shielding, centrifugal artificial gravity, in-transit consumable resupply, and a return-lander.

SpaceX and Tesla CEO Elon Musk has also announced plans to establish a colony on Mars with a population of 80,000 people. Intrinsic to this plan is the development of the Mars Colonial Transporter (MCT), a spaceflight system that would rely of reusable rocket engines, launch vehicles and space capsules to transport humans to Mars and return to Earth.

As of 2014, SpaceX has begun development of the large Raptor rocket engine for the Mars Colonial Transporter, but the MCT is not expected to be operational until the mid-2020s. In January 2015, Musk said that he hoped to release details of the "completely new architecture" for the Mars transport system in late 2015.

There may come a day when, after generations of terraforming and numerous waves of colonists, that Mars will begin to have a viable economy as well [sic]. This could take the form of mineral deposits being discovered and then sent back to Earth for sale. Launching precious metals, like platinum, off the surface of Mars would be relatively inexpensive thanks to its lower gravity.

But according to Musk, the most likely scenario (at least for the foreseeable future) would involve an economy based on real estate. With human populations exploding all over Earth, a new destination that offers plenty of room to expand is going to look like a good investment. And once transportation issues are worked out, savvy investors are likely to start buying up land.

Plus, there is likely to be a market for scientific research on Mars for centuries to come. Who knows what we might find once planetary surveys really start to open up!

In short, one day, there could be real Martians – and they would be us!

1. What makes Mars an interesting candidate for a human settlement?

2. What are some of the biggest challenges we would face in attempting to colonize Mars?

EXCERPT FROM "NASA'S JOURNEY TO MARS. PIONEERING NEXT STEPS IN SPACE EXPLORATION," FROM NASA, OCTOBER 2015

OUR GOAL

NASA aims to extend human presence deeper into the solar system and to the surface of Mars. In doing so, our human and robotic explorers will expand knowledge and discover the potential for life beyond Earth. Our goal is not bound by a single destination. We seek the capacity for people to work, learn, operate, and sustainably live safely beyond Earth for extended periods of time. We will achieve this goal with a growing number of international and commercial partners, realizing economic benefits and strengthening America's leadership on Earth and in space.

As pioneers, we seek to blaze the trail for others, establishing a presence that leads to economic progress and broad societal benefit. We pioneer space to discover life, identify resources, foster economic growth, inspire and educate, protect ourselves from space-based threats, and leave a better future for the next generation. This goal is embodied in the idea of a human and robotic journey to Mars. It is time for the next steps, and the agency is actively developing the capabilities that will enable humans to thrive beyond Earth for extended periods of time, leading to a sustainable presence in deep space.

NASA's efforts build upon the proven international and commercial partnerships at the core of the ISS. Our activities align with the Global Exploration Roadmap (GER), a product of 12 space agencies committed to expanding human presence in space. We will continue to build on partnerships with U.S. industry, academia, and our stakeholders. Our partners are developing technologies, systems, and missions to meet individual objectives, such as lunar surface operations, while contributing to the journey to Mars. The commonality between exploration capabilities, related scientific investigations, and the range of potential activities, allows partners to target individual objectives while working together to achieve pioneering goals.

While far away, Mars is a goal within our reach. We are closer to sending humans to Mars than at any point in NASA's history. We will journey in phases, leveraging our experience on the space station to step out into the Proving Ground of cislunar space—the volume of space around the moon featuring multiple stable staging orbits for future deep space missions. Over the next decade, NASA and our partners will use this Proving Ground to practice deep-space operations with decreasing reliance on the Earth, gaining the experience and systems necessary to make pioneering space and the journey to Mars a reality.

THREE PHASES ON OUR JOURNEY TO MARS

The journey to Mars passes through three thresholds, each with increasing challenges as humans move farther from Earth. NASA and our partners are managing these challenges by developing and demonstrating capabilities in incremental steps.

Earth Reliant exploration is focused on research aboard the ISS. On the space station, we are testing technologies and advancing human health and performance research that will enable deep-space, long-duration missions.

- Human health and behavioral research
- Advanced communications systems
- Material flammability tests
- Extravehicular operations
- Mars mission class environmental control and life support systems

- 3-D printing
- Material handling tests for in-situ resource utilization (ISRU) demonstrations

In the **Proving Ground**, NASA will learn to conduct complex operations in a deep space environment that allows crews to return to Earth in a matter of days. Primarily operating in cislunar space, NASA will advance and validate capabilities required for human exploration of Mars.

- A series of Exploration Missions (EMs), starting with EM-1, the first integrated test of SLS and Orion, anticipated in 2018
- The Asteroid Redirect Robotic Mission in 2020 that will collect a large boulder from a near-Earth asteroid, then ferry it to the Proving Ground and the Asteroid Redirect Crew Mission that will allow astronauts to investigate and sample the asteroid boulder
- An initial deep-space habitation facility for long-duration systems testing
- Autonomous operations, including rendezvous and docking and state of the art information technology solutions
- Concepts to minimize resupply needs through reduction, reuse, and recycling of consumables, packaging, and materials
- Other key operational capabilities required to become Earth Independent

Earth Independent activities build on what we learn on ISS and in cislunar space to enable human missions to the Mars vicinity, including the Martian moons, and eventually the Martian surface. With humans on Mars, we will be able to advance science and technology in ways only dreamed of with current robotic explorers. Future Mars missions will represent a collaborative effort among NASA and its partners—a global achievement that marks a transition in humanity's expansion as we go to Mars not just to visit, but to stay.

- Living and working within transit and surface habitats that support human life for years, with only routine maintenance
- Harvesting Martian resources to create fuel, water, oxygen, and building materials
- Leveraging advanced communication systems to relay data and results from science and exploration excursions with a 20-minute delay

OUR STRATEGY FOR THE JOURNEY TO MARS

NASA's strategy, aligned with the pioneering principles, connects near-term activities and capability development to the journey to Mars and a future with a sustainable human presence in deep space. This strategy strikes a balance between progress toward horizon goals, near-term benefits, and long-term flexibility to budgetary changes, political priorities, new scientific discoveries, technological breakthroughs, and evolving partnerships. The journey to Mars reflects an integrated NASA effort, in collaboration with our partners, to advance from today's Earth Reliant human spaceflight program through the Proving Ground of cislunar space to an Earth Independent, deep-space capability.

This strategy is a natural evolution of prior decades of space exploration. The era of modern space exploration began with remote observations through early telescopes, providing the knowledge necessary to design and send robotic missions to Earth orbit, planets, moons, comets, and asteroids. NASA's human spaceflight program has already demonstrated the capability for Earth Reliant human exploration, culminating today with the ISS, where astronauts and supplies are ferried between the station and Earth within hours. Our partners on the ISS, which now include commercial spaceflight ventures, reflect a blossoming worldwide human spaceflight capability for low Earth orbit (LEO). Meanwhile, robotic science missions are scouting resources and characterizing potential destinations for human explorers at far more distant locations within our solar system.

What Is Pioneering?

Pioneering space requires a sustained set of mutually reinforcing activities—science missions, technology development, capability demonstrations, and human spaceflight—to expand human presence into deep space and extend our robotic agents farther into the solar system, with the horizon goal of humans traveling to Mars and remaining on the surface.

THE PATH FORWARD

NASA and our partners are already at Mars, operating with highly effective robotic emissaries in orbit and on the surface. NASA has exploited nearly every opportunity over the past two decades (occurring every 26 months when transit between Earth and Mars is the most efficient) to send orbiters, landers, and rovers to the Red Planet with increasingly complex experiments and sensing systems. Mars orbiters have mapped with high precision the topography of the planet, begun mapping the distribution of water ice below the surface, imaged geologically ancient river deltas, and discovered likely seasonal outflows of salty liquid water in the present. They have mapped detailed mineral composition in select areas and located suitable landing sites for future robotic and human missions, many with incredible science potential. Robotic landers have demonstrated that the Martian environment could have supported microbial life, as we understand it here on Earth. Additionally, robotic landers have measured radiation in transit and on the surface, and gathered data for defining entry, descent, and landing (EDL) approaches for future human missions. NASA's Mars 2020 mission will measure atmospheric entry conditions and surface dust, and demonstrate production of oxygen from atmospheric carbon dioxide while selecting and encapsulating samples for potential return to Earth. The journey to Mars requires advanced human and robotic partnerships not imagined at the time of Apollo.

While learning about Mars with robotic science scouts, we are also developing advanced technologies to support human pioneers. NASA is investing in technologies and rapidly prototyping new systems, which benefit both NASA and our industry partners, while minimizing overall costs through innovative partnerships. Focus areas include solar electric propulsion with advanced ion thrusters, habitation systems, nuclear fission for Mars surface power, EDL systems, laser communications for high data rate transmission, deep-space atomic clocks for precise navigation, and many others. NASA will integrate these technologies into pioneering capabilities, providing the tools necessary for the journey to Mars.

MOVING FROM EARTH RELIANT TOWARD EARTH INDEPENDENT

In the current Earth Reliant phase of human exploration, NASA and our partners are using the ISS in LEO, supported by commercial cargo resupply services and in the near future, commercial crew transportation. The delivery and return of astronauts and cargo to the space station are measured in hours, but any journey to Mars will take many months each way, and early return is not an option. This is an entirely different operating regime, not just for physical access but also for communications with Earth-based teams. Astronauts in deep space must be more self-reliant and spacecraft systems and operations must be more automated to operate safely and productively as we explore beyond LEO. Cislunar space is the ideal Proving Ground for NASA and its partners to test systems and to practice deep-space operations, such as extra-vehicular activity (EVAs or spacewalks), and rendezvous and docking prior to committing crew on long missions to Mars. NASA is focusing on Proving Ground activities in cislunar space, and many of our partners see cislunar space as a step toward human missions to the lunar surface. These combined activities provide an optimal condition to demonstrate integrated human and robotic missions to build confidence that human missions to Mars can be safely conducted with an Earth Independent mode of operation.

OUR STRATEGY FOR THE JOURNEY TO MARS

Living and working in space require accepting risk, and the journey is worth the risk. Crews must be protected from the unique hazardous environments of deep space and on the Martian surface. Often, systems will have to operate autonomously or remain dormant for years in preparation for crew. Overcoming these challenges will be essential on the journey to Mars. These technological and operational challenges fall into three categories: transportation, sending humans and cargo through space efficiently, safely, and reliably; working in space, enabling productive operations for crew and robotic systems; and staying healthy, developing habitation systems that provide safe, healthy, and sustainable human exploration. Bridging these three categories are the overarching logistical challenges facing crewed missions lasting up to 1,100 days and exploration campaigns that span decades.

PLANNING AND IMPLEMENTING A PIONEERING APPROACH

A pioneering approach enables a sustained expansion of human presence into the solar system, rather than a once-in-a-generation expedition. This approach requires us to recognize and address two key challenges. The first challenge is recognition that pioneering space is as much a logistics and supply chain challenge as a technological challenge. Historically, pioneers on Earth could not rely solely on supplies from home to sustain them and neither can the first pioneers on Mars. NASA will have to learn new ways of operating in space, based on self-reliance and increased system reliability; ISRU, including recycling packaging materials and trash; and the ability to design, build, or repair systems with common, modular components. To enable the journey to Mars, NASA will invest in reusable systems with common components that are modular and extensible to multiple missions to reduce unique developments and the need for spares. Complex tradeoffs between resupply and use of insitu resources must be first addressed before we achieve Earth Independence. NASA will use missions in the Proving Ground to validate new operational approaches and learn how to balance logistics sent from Earth with the potential benefits and challenges of using local resources.

The second challenge is recognition that achieving Earth Independence will take decades and can be impacted by multiple uncertain events. NASA's strategy must be flexible and resilient to changes in the priorities of future administrations, the emergence of breakthrough technologies, discovery of new scientific knowledge, fluctuations in funding, and new partnership opportunities. Due to these uncertainties, we must make decisions with incomplete knowledge to ensure continued momentum. However, we can plan for these changes proactively and design for uncertainty to be better positioned when change occurs. We do this by designing a resilient architecture that focuses on critical capabilities across a range of potential missions, investing in technologies that provide large returns, and maximizing flexibility and adaptability through commonality, modularity, and reusability. The journey to Mars is only possible through multi-use, evolvable space infrastructure that minimizes unique developments and associated cost. We also ensure each mission leaves something behind to reduce the cost, risk, or schedule for the next mission.

OUR PROGRESS AND PLANS ON THE JOURNEY TO MARS

NASA's current efforts focus on strategic investments to extend human access to deep space, learn how to operate with reduced logistics, and understand future destinations through science-guided robotic explorers. We will use the Proving Ground to demonstrate capabilities that evolve beyond the Earth Reliant exploration systems currently used on the ISS. As these capabilities are proven, NASA and our partners will further define future missions. Efforts made today and in the next decade will lay the foundation for an Earth Independent, sustained presence in deep space, addressing a challenge worthy of our nation's expertise, perseverance, and ingenuity.

The following sections describe specific architecture elements in each phase of the journey to Mars: Earth Reliant, Proving Ground, and Earth Independent. These investments, selected with guidance from strategic partners and through the lens of the pioneering principles, enable near-term missions, support resilient space infrastructure, are affordable within NASA's current budget, and offer multiple opportunities for academic, commercial, and international partnerships. They work together as an interlocking set of capabilities that enable sustainable, affordable, programmatically sound, and technically feasible architecture. Additional detail is provided for the first series of exploration missions, including initial SLS and Orion missions and the Asteroid Redirect Mission. For missions beyond the next decade, insight from ongoing studies is provided.

EARTH RELIANT

NASA's current human exploration activities occur in an Earth Reliant frame of operations on the ISS. To begin to break these ties, NASA is leveraging the space station as a test bed to demonstrate key exploration capabilities and operations. Current NASA missions are building on the Earth Reliant capabilities to enable missions for the next decade. The agency is also facilitating a robust commercial crew and cargo transportation capability in LEO, stimulating new markets and fostering an emerging commercial space industry that will mature to support future pioneering missions. As NASA transitions beyond LEO and continues to pioneer space, our vision is that private and public investments will sustain economic activity in LEO and create benefits for Earth through commercial supply and public and private demand.

THE FIRST STEPS: INTERNATIONAL SPACE STATION (ISS)

NASA has begun the transition from exploration to pioneering on the ISS. Occupied by an international crew continuously since November 2, 2000, the station has hosted more than 200 people from 17 countries, and is the culmination of one of the largest and most complicated international engineering efforts ever attempted.

The ISS is the only microgravity platform for the long-term testing of new life support and crew health systems, advanced habitat modules, and other technologies needed to decrease reliance on Earth. Over the next decade, we will validate many of the capabilities needed to maintain a healthy and productive crew in deep space. Currently manifested or planned experiments and demonstrations include improved long-duration life support for Mars missions, advanced fire safety equipment, next-generation spacesuit technologies, high-data-rate communications, techniques to reduce logistics, large deployable solar arrays, in-space additive manufacturing, advanced exercise and medical equipment, radiation monitoring and shielding, humanrobotic operations, and autonomous crew operations.

Aboard the ISS, NASA and its partners also conduct targeted research to improve our understanding of how humans adapt and function during long-duration space travel. Current and planned risk-reducing investigations include bone and muscle loss studies, understanding the effects of intracranial pressure changes and fluid shifts, monitoring immune function and cardiovascular health, conducting nutritional studies, and validating exercise protocols. With these studies, NASA explores the physiology of the human body, preparing for long-duration spaceflight and supporting development of terrestrial drugs and therapeutic practices. NASA and our partners' activities on the ISS are achieving key milestones and enabling a planned transition to early pioneering missions in cislunar space.

The guiding principles for pioneering space include leveraging non-NASA capabilities and partnering with industry whenever possible. NASA's acquisition strategy for commercial crew and cargo services embodies these principles. The ISS plays a key role as a destination and anchor customer for emerging commercial markets in LEO. Commercial partners, who are maturing their business models and technical approaches by providing critical services for the ISS, will be essential to enabling deep-space NASA missions.

The NASA-sponsored Commercial Orbital Transportation Services (COTS) program resulted in the development of new launch vehicles and cargo spacecraft. Both Space Exploration Technologies (SpaceX) and Orbital ATK have successfully delivered cargo to the ISS using vehicles developed with NASA support. Under the Commercial Resupply Services (CRS) and followon contracts, commercial partners are expected to provide about six flights per year to support ISS operations. These flights are win-win arrangements for NASA and industry, as they minimize the need for costly, NASA-unique infrastructure and increase commercial access to space.

In September 2014, NASA announced the next phase of the commercial services program, Commercial Crew Transportation Capability (CCtCap), under which NASA awarded contracts for crew transportation services to Boeing and SpaceX. Once the companies complete development and are certified by NASA, the agency will purchase two flights per year to deliver and return expedition crew. CCtCap will provide NASA and our international partners with additional vehicles to deliver crews to the ISS and expand research opportunities by enabling the crew aboard ISS to increase from six to seven. NASA also continues relationships with other U.S. companies that are developing alternative transportation systems.

Beyond commercial crew and cargo transportation services, NASA is also developing strategies to stimulate sustained economic activity in LEO. This includes leveraging the ISS; supporting a policy and regulatory environment that promotes commercialization of LEO; facilitating a robust, self-sustaining, and cost-effective supply of U.S. commercial services that accommodates public and private demands; and stimulating broad sectors of the economy discovering benefits of LEO.

NASA is also leveraging industry to reinvent ground operations for a flexible, multiuser spaceport, providing launch services for both government and commercial partners. Launch complex assets once used for the space shuttle have been modernized for next-generation transportation systems. Many of these assets also provide opportunities for the commercial space industry. For example, Boeing's Crew Space Transportation (CST)-100 Starliner commercial spacecraft is processed in the former NASA orbiter processing facility, and SpaceX plans to use Launch Complex 39A, a former space shuttle launch pad, for commercial heavy-lift launch vehicles. These and other innovative commercial partnerships have reshaped the way NASA provides launch services through a multi-user spaceport.

Over the next 10 years, commercial partners will likely increase their presence in LEO by providing more products and services to government and nongovernmental customers. A mature market provides reliable, on-demand, low-cost services, freeing NASA resources for more complex missions and system development. These commercial service providers help NASA execute an ambitious deep-space human exploration strategy within the agency's anticipated budgets.

THE PROVING GROUND

Starting early next decade, NASA will be part of a larger international community of exploration and commercial activity in the Proving Ground—a resilient, evolvable effort to extend human presence beyond LEO. NASA identified several objectives for Proving Ground missions, which are critical steps on the journey to Mars. These objectives range from demonstrating advanced solar electric propulsion (SEP) for interplanetary cargo transportation to in-space operations and deep-space habitation. New missions and activities will become possible as NASA and its partners validate capabilities, address Proving Ground objectives, and review the specific series of near-term missions. Through these missions, we are moving toward Earth Independence and progressing together on the journey to Mars.

A ROBUST TRANSPORTATION INFRASTRUCTURE: GROUND OPERATIONS, ORION, AND SLS

NASA is developing a robust launch services capability, which not only supports SLS and Orion, but can also be leveraged by a multitude of new commercial launch providers. With commercial partners, the agency is modernizing Launch Complex 39B, developing a mobile launcher, upgrading control systems, and demonstrating ground processing capabilities to enable Proving Ground missions, including the launch of SLS and Orion.

Orion is a launch, reentry, and in-space crew spacecraft designed to transport a crew of four to deep space. During Proving Ground missions, Orion will protect the crew during transport to cislunar space, sustain the crew for short durations while in space, and enable safe reentry. For future missions, Orion will provide transportation between Earth and the Mars transit systems located in cislunar space. Orion's first mission, Exploration Flight Test 1 (EFT-1), was successfully conducted in 2014, on a Delta IV Heavy launch vehicle, and generated a wealth of data to enable future human missions to deep space.

The Space Launch System is Orion's ride to deep space. NASA is developing an evolvable design for SLS that leverages previous launch system investments. The initial "Block 1" SLS is designed to carry Orion, as well as cargo, equipment, and science experiments to staging points in cislunar space. We are well along the path to developing the Block 1 SLS, which uses an upper stage derived from the Delta cryogenic second stage to launch 70 metric tons (mt) to orbit. This initial version will use liquid hydrogen and liquid oxygen propulsion systems and solid rocket boosters, evolved from heritage systems. NASA plans to upgrade the boosters and develop an advanced upper stage, the Exploration Upper Stage (EUS), leading to the 105 mt Block 1B and the 130 mt Block 2 versions of the SLS. This payload capacity far exceeds the capability of current and planned commercial launch vehicles. Development of Block 1B with the EUS provides significant additional capability for Proving Ground missions, allowing NASA to send the crewed Orion spacecraft, other flight systems, and cargo to lunar orbit in a single launch. Additional developments will improve SLS performance and reduce manufacturing costs through additive manufacturing and advanced out-of-autoclave composite structures.

The initial Block 1 SLS will support the first deep-space exploration mission, Exploration Mission 1 (EM-1), anticipated in 2018. Although uncrewed, EM-1 will provide the first integrated test of SLS and Orion, including SLS's launch performance, Orion's heat shield, and deep-space navigation. NASA plans to develop the EUS for early exploration missions to cislunar space. The EUS addition could provide SLS with a critical new capability for crewed Orion missions by allowing secondary payloads to be co-manifested within the EUS-to-Orion launch vehicle adapter. While the exact mass and volume available for co-manifested payloads have not yet been determined, payloads about the same length, twice the width, and one-third the mass of a school bus could be launched to cislunar space with Orion. Co-manifested payloads, potentially launched as early as Exploration Mission 2 (EM-2), could include pressurized modules that extend the deep-space capabilities of the Orion spacecraft and help develop a deep-space habitation capability. Independent co-manifested payloads, such as robotic science missions, are also possible.

Orion and SLS (with the EUS) provide the core transportation capabilities that support Proving Ground missions and enable the journey to Mars. Beyond EM-2,

NASA is considering a wide range of activities that not only demonstrate the ability to live and work in deep space, but also accomplish a suite of Proving Ground objectives and validate key operational capabilities required to become Earth Independent. While SLS and Orion flight rates will ultimately be determined by available funding and mission requirements, NASA is working towards flying at least one crewed mission per year.

INTO THE PROVING GROUND: SOLAR ELECTRIC PROPULSION AND THE ASTEROID REDIRECT MISSION

Solar electric propulsion (SEP) uses energy from the sun to accelerate ionized propellant to very high speeds. Compared to chemical propulsion, electric propulsion provides very low levels of thrust; however, it is incredibly efficient and can provide thrust continuously for months or years, allowing more mass to be transported with far less propellant. These systems are an order of magnitude more efficient than chemical propulsion systems, with a specific impulse (Isp) from 2,000-3,000 seconds compared to 200-500 seconds. SEP systems are also very resilient and, if refueled, could provide a reusable, in-space transportation infrastructure. Adding a SEP capability to Orion and SLS provides a robust transportation infrastructure for human missions to support the journey to Mars.

High-power SEP is a key enabler for NASA's pioneering strategy, allowing NASA to pre-position infrastructure and resources while reducing the surge of launches. This could reduce the costs estimated in previous human Mars mission studies. Pre-positioning supplies months or years ahead of crew, rather than aggregating all necessary equipment and supplies in Earth orbit, is often called a split mission. With several tons of xenon (Xe) propellant and solar arrays capable of generating 40 kilowatts (kW), an early SEP vehicle could efficiently position several tons of cargo throughout the solar system. A more advanced SEP system with additional power and propellant could deliver landers, habitats, and supplies to Mars orbit.

NASA is considering several mission architectures that evolve from a 40 kW SEP vehicle. In an approach that leverages both SEP and chemical propulsion, a Mars SEP cargo vehicle would transport chemical return stages, habitats, and landers to Mars orbit, while crew travel separately. For this approach, the crew would rendezvous with the pre-positioned assets in Mars orbit including a surface lander and, on the return trip to Earth, chemical departure stages. In an alternative approach, NASA would use a hybrid SEP vehicle, supplemented with small chemical engines for strategic high-thrust maneuvers, to reduce trip times. This vehicle would still pre-position landers, habitats, and equipment in a cargo mode; however, for crew transit, the vehicle would contain enough propellant for a round trip and would not require chemical return stages. Both approaches are being studied as the Mars transportation architecture evolves.

With SEP, NASA can also aggregate, refurbish, and reuse Mars transportation infrastructure in a high-energy orbit, such as lunar distant retrograde orbit (LDRO). High performance liquid oxygen and hydrogen propulsion from the SLS Exploration Upper Stage can provide the majority of departure energy, placing payloads in these high-energy orbits and allowing the SEP or SEPhybrid thrusters to initiate the maneuver to Mars. As an added advantage, these maneuvers can be reversed, allowing NASA to capture the Mars return vehicle for refurbishment and reuse. Developing and demonstrating advanced SEP systems early during the Proving Ground missions will accelerate our progress toward sustainable pioneering.

The Asteroid Redirect Mission (ARM) provides a near-term opportunity to demonstrate several capabilities important for longer-duration, deep-space missions, including flight-validated SEP transportation. ARM consists of two challenging flight segments, working toward the common objective of human exploration of an asteroid. In the first segment, an advanced, high-power SEP robotic vehicle will travel to an asteroid, perform detailed reconnaissance of its surface, select a boulder-sized sample, capture it, and return to a stable orbit in cislunar space. Most robotic sample return concepts are designed to return a few hundred grams of material (e.g., NASA's OSIRIS-REx mission to the asteroid Bennu). All six Apollo landings returned a total of less than 400 kilograms. Leveraging SEP and advanced robotics, ARM will return several tons of material. In the second segment, astronauts will travel to the captured boulder aboard SLS and Orion, marking a historic opportunity that will allow humans to venture outside of the spacecraft to touch, investigate, and experience an asteroid firsthand.

The Asteroid Redirect Mission also leaves deep-space infrastructure in cislunar space, providing an aggregation point to support the journey to Mars. Following the first ARM crewed mission, there will be on the order of several tons of material remaining in a stable orbit for at least 100 years, available for future exploration, scientific, commercial, or academic partners. During potential future missions, NASA could use the boulder to demonstrate ISRU identification, characterization, extraction, processing, and containment capabilities, and test EVA tools for exploring other low-gravity bodies, such as the Martian moons Phobos and Deimos. The Asteroid Redirect Robotic Vehicle (ARRV) also will be able to provide some support to visiting vehicles, including an S-band transponder for approach and docking, an X-band communications link, and about 40 kW of power. This initial cislunar infrastructure would be available to commercial partners who may also wish to understand and eventually mine resources from asteroids. Such commercial efforts could evolve into services to support in-space fueling of Mars propulsion systems.

A HOME AWAY FROM HOME: DEEP-SPACE HABITAT

Any mission to Mars will require highly reliable habitation systems to keep the crew healthy and productive in the deep-space environment during missions that last up to 1,100 days. Leveraging experience from the ISS, NASA and our international and commercial partners have begun activities to evolve ISS habitation systems to meet future deep-space mission needs. With multiple crewed Orion missions to cislunar space over the next decade (launched on an evolved SLS), NASA will have many opportunities to use these habitations systems, and evolve them to a deep-space habitation capability for future Mars missions. This approach allows us to validate habitation system performance and reliability in the deep-space environment prior to committing a crew on a long journey to Mars.

NASA, together with its international and commercial partners, will develop a strategy to complete "Mars-ready" habitation system testing on Earth and on ISS. NASA and its partners will also develop an initial habitation capability for short-duration missions in cislunar space during the early 2020s and evolve this capability for long-duration missions in the later 2020s. A modular, pressurized volume would enable extended stays by crews arriving with Orion. This initial habitation capability in cislunar space would demonstrate all the capabilities and countermeasures necessary to send humans on long-duration transit missions to Mars. With this long-duration habitable volume and resources, NASA and its partners will have the opportunity to validate Mars habitat concepts and systems, including exercise systems, environmental monitoring systems, longduration consumables storage, fire safety in high-oxygen environments, radiation shielding, and high-reliability avionics with long periods of dormancy. Understanding the transition from dormancy to crew presence and back is particularly important and can be tested with this capability. Between crewed missions, deep-space habitation capabilities could be used to test autonomous mission operations and transfer of control from the ground to vehicle systems in preparation for the longer Mars missions. Many of the capabilities developed for NASA's deep space missions will also be useful for other missions—including potential future commercial low Earth orbit space stations used by other government agencies and the private sector as the agency transitions away from the Space Station after 2024.

As designs for the Mars transit vehicle evolve and trajectories are determined, future Proving Ground

missions could launch additional modules to incremen-
tally build up capability. Using standardized interfaces,
common structures, and modular designs, multiple
pressure vessels could be aggregated, leading to a
more complete habitation system to validate the full
suite of capabilities needed for the journey to Mars.
Commonality and standardization reduce unique
developments and improve logistical efficiency.
Standards also increase opportunities for international and commercial partnerships. During the habitat
build-up and after initial missions, outdated or failing
systems could be replaced with new capabilities that
leverage the standardized interfaces. This approach
provides an initial cislunar exploration capability with
a pathway to a reusable, evolvable infrastructure for
human missions to Mars.

BECOMING EARTH INDEPENDENT

Part of the journey to Mars is increasing our knowledge base and assessing plans and architectures that
are affordable and sustainable. When the first pioneers ventured to North America, they found familiar
resources in the new land and adapted to their environment. Future pioneers of Mars will have to adapt to
a more foreign, hostile environment. We will need new
technologies to transform local resources into water,
fuel, air, and building materials. Therefore, in parallel
with planning and implementing Proving Ground missions, NASA is leveraging current and planned robotic
missions and studies to better understand challenges
and opportunities that will inform the design of future

systems. Earth Independent capabilities include those validated in the Proving Ground, Mars surface landers, advanced and efficient ISRU, surface mobility, permanent surface habitats, and crew transfer vehicles, such as the Mars ascent vehicle or a Mars vicinity crew taxi. These capabilities enable an integrated and sustainable campaign to pioneer space.

ON THE RED PLANET: ROBOTIC MARS MISSIONS

We are already in orbit around and on the surface of Mars with a fleet of robotic science explorers. Robotic pathfinders like Curiosity address both science and human exploration objectives, answering key questions and gathering knowledge necessary to prepare human pioneers. NASA has significant experience using robotic science and exploration pathfinders, such as the Lunar Reconnaissance Orbiter (LRO) mission to the moon, the Dawn mission to asteroids Vesta and Ceres, and the Mars Exploration Rovers Spirit and Opportunity. Along with conducting their high-priority science objectives, robotic pathfinders investigate and map destinations prior to human missions, collect surface samples, characterize potential landing sites, and test technologies necessary for future robotic and human destination systems. Over the next decade, NASA will rely on robotic pathfinders to help select human-accessible landing sites, pre-emplace infrastructure, and inform the design of human destination systems.

PIONEERING CHALLENGES

NASA has identified specific scientific and technical challenges for the journey to Mars through rigorous studies, including an ongoing series of architectural trade analyses, external reviews, assessments of deep-space habitation options with international partners, and high-priority objectives of science decadal studies. NASA and our partners around the world have already solved some of these challenges. The remaining challenges will be systematically addressed over the next two decades by the capabilities demonstrated through science missions, on the ISS, and in the Proving Ground as we move toward Earth Independence.

TRANSPORTATION

Transportation capabilities are necessary to send humans to space affordably and reliably, provide high-thrust access to staging points in cislunar space, and efficiently and safely transport crew and exploration systems on the longer journey to Mars.

Commercial Cargo and Crew: Advances in transportation capabilities are only possible if NASA can shift to a more efficient mode of operations for current Earth-to-LEO transportation. NASA is partnering with commercial industry to make this shift possible. Through a commercial crew and cargo capability, NASA can rely on a less expensive, flexible commercial market to provide LEO transportation services, freeing up resources for beyond LEO and planetary transportation.

Beyond Low Earth Orbit Propulsion—SLS and Orion: A human-class Mars mission will require unprecedented amounts of mass transported farther than any previous human mission to space. A single Mars mission may require several 20-30 mt payloads delivered to the surface to support the crew as well as an in-space habitat, transportation stages, and supplies for round-trip missions of up to 1,100-days. In addition to mass, payload volume is a challenge. To enable cargo missions, NASA envisions a new 10-meter diameter fairing for the evolved SLS to accommodate unprecedented volumes. Commercial cargo services may be used to supplement the SLS's core role.

In-Space Power and Propulsion: Power is critical for exploration systems; however, it is particularly important for the transportation architecture. Each human Mars mission will require several cargo launches to pre-emplace infrastructure and supplies. NASA expects to use high-powered SEP systems (150-200 kW) that can transport cargo in a sustainable cadence. SEP requires 50 percent less propellant than chemical propulsion and uses fewer heavy-lift launches. While SEP takes longer than chemical propulsion to deliver cargo, it gives campaign planners more timeline flexibility by providing trajectory options that are less coupled to the 26-month planetary alignment that drives traditional chemical propulsion architectures.

Entry, Descent, and Landing: EDL is one of our biggest challenges. The revolutionary sky crane landing system used for the Curiosity rover placed just under 1 mt of payload on the surface of Mars. The smallest viable human-scale lander concept is more than an order of magnitude larger, and it may be necessary to land multiple 20-30 mt payloads at a human landing site. Consequently, a completely new approach is needed for human-scale EDL. For instance, supersonic retropropulsion may be necessary to provide safe and accurate atmospheric entry, descent, and precision landing on Mars.

Ascent from Planetary Surfaces: A Mars Ascent Vehicle (MAV) is required to transport crews from the surface to Mars orbit. The MAV drives lander and EDL requirements, which in turn impact in-space propulsion and the total mass launched from Earth, a major driver for mission cost. Current MAV designs require a minimum lander size of just under 20 mt, assuming propellant can be generated from the Martian atmosphere via ISRU. The MAV is also critical to crew survival, requiring additional reliability and redundancy, zero boil-off cryogenic storage, and limited maintenance during years of dormancy. Current studies continue to refine our understanding of this critical element.

Communication and Navigation: Currently, Mars robotic rovers have data rates around two million bits per second, using a relay, such as the Mars Reconnaissance Orbiter. The ISS data rate is 300 million bits per second, two orders of magnitude faster. Future human Mars missions may need up to a billion bits per second at 1,000 times greater range than ISS, requiring laser communications to reduce weight and power. In addition, disruption and error-tolerant interplanetary networking and improved navigation capabilities are required to ensure accurate trajectories and precision landing.

STAYING HEALTHY

Deep-space crewed missions will not have regular access to the Earth's resources or the ability to rapidly return to Earth if a system fails. As crewed missions extend farther from Earth for longer periods, the habitation systems must become more reliable for safe, healthy, and sustainable human exploration.

Environmental Control and Life Support Systems (ECLSS): Leveraging the ISS, NASA is focused on demonstrating advanced capabilities for robust and reliable ECLSS, which must operate for up to 1,100 days with minimal spares and consumables. Systems demonstrated on the ISS and Orion will be further validated in the Proving Ground environment and incorporated into a reliable long-duration, deep-space habitation capability.

Crew Health: Long-duration human missions, including missions with up to 1,100 days in microgravity, potentially increase the risks of bone loss, atrophy, trauma, neurovestibular issues, loss of clear vision, and illness for the crew. To address these increased risks, crews will require new diagnostic, monitoring, and treatment tools and techniques, including exercise systems and other countermeasures, to maintain crew health. The ISS provides an ideal test bed to develop these capabilities.

Radiation Safety: Outside the Earth's magnetic field, crew and electronics are exposed to high-energy particles, including infrequent, but potentially deadly, solar particle events and constant exposure to galactic cosmic rays. These high-energy particles can reduce immune response, increase cancer risk, and interfere with electronics. NASA's Human Research Program is developing methods and technologies to protect, mitigate, and treat the effects of radiation on the crew and their exploration systems.

The journey to Mars will be further defined through Proving Ground missions in the next decade, as NASA and our partners retire these challenges and build on the capabilities for sustainable pioneering. We know these challenges are solvable and have a strategy in place for maturing the capabilities to address them as we expand human presence into deep space.

SUMMARY

We are on a journey to Mars. In the next few decades, NASA will take steps toward establishing a sustainable human presence beyond Earth, not just to visit but to stay. NASA's near-term activities focus on increasing our capacity to operate, work, and live in space while characterizing future destinations with the help of robotic science missions. Pioneering space begins with the ISS to ensure we have the reliable, long-duration systems necessary for human missions to Mars. In the Proving Ground, we will validate key capabilities through EM-1 and EM-2 along with ARM, SEP, cislunar habitation, and long-duration testing and operations. These and subsequent missions will target challenges and strategic knowledge gaps while helping develop the core capabilities necessary to expand human activity farther into deep space.

Pioneering space will require a flexible, integrated, and sustained effort to develop the capabilities and tools necessary to support humans throughout our solar system. Future missions will face increasingly difficult challenges associated with *transportation, working in space, and staying healthy*. Many of these challenges are solved or are currently being addressed on the ISS. For the rest, NASA and our partners will leverage the Proving Ground with science missions and capability demonstrations to close the remaining gaps and ensure we have the ability to get to Mars, land safely, live and work productively, and return.

NASA's strategy for pioneering space provides guidance for selecting and designing missions in the Proving Ground and enables future accomplishments on the journey to Mars. The strategy helps NASA logically progress from current Earth Reliant operations on the ISS, through the Proving Ground in cislunar space, to Earth Independent pioneering with the goal of humans living and working on Mars. This strategy provides the flexibility to respond to new discoveries, opportunities, and shifts in national priorities. NASA approaches pioneering space as a collaborative effort, within the United States and with our international partners, incorporating key capabilities from industry and academia, while engaging the public and stakeholder communities. The core capabilities NASA is working on with our partners—SEP, Mars-ready ECLSS, ISRU, and many more—will enable the journey to Mars.

NASA's human exploration, science, and technology endeavors are intertwined. As our exploration activities reach farther into the solar system, we will also broaden our reach here on Earth, enabling more participation, partners, activity, and economic and technological benefits. NASA's current investments in exploration capabilities and the decisions being made today are crucial to

achieving our common goal: extending human presence
into the solar system and to the surface of Mars.

1. What do you think of NASA's three-phase strategy
   to Mars? Is this an attainable strategy?

2. How would you plan an actual mission to Mars?

"FAILURE TO LAUNCH: THE TECHNICAL, ETHICAL, AND LEGAL CASE AGAINST MARS ONE," BY MICHAEL LISTNER AND CHRISTOPHER NEWMAN, FROM *THE SPACE REVIEW*, MARCH 16, 2015

The Mars One Project is the brainchild of Dutch entrepreneur Bas Lansdorp. The proposition is seemingly a
simple one: select a team of four volunteers to establish a permanently colony on Mars with a launch date of
2024. Given that this will be, according to Lansdorp "the
media event of the century," the $6-billion venture will
be funded in part by a reality TV show and subsequent
media sponsorship.

Undoubtedly, Mars One has captured the zeit-
geist with disproportionately optimistic media coverage
heralding the selection of a group of hopeful colonists. Yet,
significant criticisms and troubling questions encircle the

project. This article will examine those questions and criticisms and provide a sobering evaluation of some of the technical, legal and ethical challenges facing Mars One. This article is not intended to be an exhaustive examination of all the technical, ethical, legal, and political issues facing this venture. Rather it is intended to be a précis of some of the issues that need to be addressed by the Mars One Project if it to meet its deadline and its goals.

At the outset, there are two important and interlinked caveats that preface this discussion. First, it should be noted many of the problems facing the Mars One project are not *sui generis* to this endeavor. Any crewed mission to Mars will face them. The issue is not that such problems are insurmountable; merely that Mars One does not have the capacity or the budget for the research and development necessary to overcome them. Second, and perhaps crucially, this is not an attack on the people involved in the project. There is much to admire in the pioneering spirit and genuine enthusiasm held by those involved. This discussion is not seeking to discredit or diminish their bold vision. It is the project itself that is under scrutiny, a project that poses significant risk to these participants.

CLUTCHING AT STRAWS: THE ILLUSION OF EXISTING TECHNOLOGY

Although the ethical and legal challenges facing Mars One are considerable, this venture will ultimately rise or fall on the technical and engineering elements. The stated aim of Mars One, according to their website, is to use "existing technologies available from proven suppliers."(1) This statement provides the first crucial difficulty. At each crucial phase of the mission—travel to Mars, landing, and establishing a permanent colony—the claim that of utilizing existing technology is unsustainable.

For example, at present the only existing operational human spaceflight vehicle is the Russian Soyuz capsule. Mars One states that the existing technology that will be used to traverse millions of kilometers from the Earth to Mars will instead be a variant of SpaceX's Dragon capsule. To call the considerable research and development that this would require as "existing technology" is, at best, grossly oversimplifying the issue.

The Mars One project also provides no detail in respect of the development of reliable and effective life support systems and the problematic subject of dealing with human waste disposal. These are issues that will ultimately need to be solved for a successful mission to Mars, and there is significant research and development activity ongoing in this area. (2) Such technology is, however, by no means "existing" without a significant amount of investment in research and development.

The picture is very much the same when considering the critical issue of landing the Mars One colonists on the Martian surface. Considered one of the most problematic aspects of human exploration, it is this aspect of the Mars One project where the notion of using existing technology is exposed as being dangerously misleading. The existing technology that has landed rovers on Mars is inadequate for landing humans. (3) The Martian atmosphere poses considerable and serious challenges for landing a heavy payload onto the surface. The atmosphere varies considerably, making it extremely difficult to scale up existing technology used to land small rovers. Supersonic retropropulsion, which at present seems the most promising method of overcoming the obstacles posed by the variable Martian atmosphere, still requires expensive research and development. (4) Again, this is not a problem unique to the Mars One project. It is, however, a fundamental obstacle to a 2023 mission with a projected budget of $6 billion.

Assuming, however, that the Mars One crew successfully makes it to the Martian surface, one aspect of space technology that remains untested, and makes the Mars One project fundamentally different from any previous space activity, is the technology required for the permanent settlement of Mars. Much has been made of in situ resource utilization (ISRU) technologies that will enable the colonists to live off the land. The much-publicized MIT feasibility study of Mars One casts significant doubt on the readiness of this technology, none of which has been deployed in practice. (5) When challenged on this, the Mars One team responded by maintaining that the MIT study was based on ISS operations and therefore the study does not provide a valid comparison. (6)

Such assertions are, however, inconsistent with the stated aim of using existing technology. Either Mars One will utilize existing technology that has been tested in space on the ISS (in which case the MIT study is valid), or they will be looking to extrapolate new, untested methods of ISRU, which raises questions of reliability and cost in terms of money and time. In any event, the MIT study did not consider issues such as establishing a reliable power system and communications network, as well as the costly issue of spacesuit and habitat development. All these issues raise further questions about the technical feasibility of the entire venture.

The funding model for the Mars One project has already been criticized as being flawed. (7) A trip to Mars is not simply "Apollo with bigger rockets" (8) and, on a crude costing basis, the Apollo program cost the modern-day equivalent of $100 billion. (9) What the Apollo program did demonstrate unequivocally was that pioneering developmental space exploration almost invariably exceeds even the most generous budgetary estimates. Simply put, the figures do not suggest Mars One has anywhere near the requisite resource base to accomplish even the most fundamental research and development required for an undertaking of this nature.

THE ETHICAL VACUUM: MARS ONE, PSYCHOLOGY, AND EXPERIMENTATION

Perhaps more significant that the technical issues with Mars One, though, is the deficit in understanding the human dynamic of a one-way trip to Mars. This has been identified by many as posing a danger to the crew that is every bit as deadly as the technical problems. (10) Psychologists have already highlighted serious threats to mental health such as social isolation, confinement and lack of direct access to mental health services. (11) Unfortunately, the funding model of Mars One actually serves to exacerbate these difficulties by adding a loss of privacy to the already potent mix. The Russian Mars 500 experiment clearly established that there was a threat to mental health from prolonged space travel. (12)

Such issues point to three fundamental ethical difficulties. First, it is unclear how a crewmember suffering a severe mental health issue will be dealt with in respect of privacy. Reality TV demands spectacle, and sponsors who are paying large sums of money will be dependent on incident once the drama of launch and landing has abated. The humane and ethical course of action would be to suspend TV coverage whilst the psychological support team tried to manage the incident, but TV executives may well be tempted to exploit this situation. Will counseling sessions be televised? The impact of such fundamental invasion of privacy, under the most extreme and trying conditions, is simply not understood. There has been no clear and detailed plan articulating the way in which the mental health of the crew will be monitored.

The necessary psychological interventions described above will be made substantially more difficult as it is not in real time, given the communications delay. The Mars One project website has a FAQ site which specifically deals with health and ethics, but there is no specific information provided on what will be televised and what will not. (13) Simply reiterating that the potential colonists are "living their dream" is no substitute for a robust consideration of the significant threats posed to the mental health of those who volunteer for Mars One. This ethical concern gives rise to a fundamental issue of liability for the welfare of the crew and the conditions in which they will live. Psychologist Chris Chalmers highlights this fundamental flaw in the project:

> The notion that "attitude" will somehow inoculate the colonists against these conditions is at best naive, at worst irresponsible. How will the

Mars One program react when a colonist who was
deemed psychologically fit suffers a major break-
down after years of isolation, with no way to get
home? Who will be responsible then? (14)

The second significant ethical difficulty is linked in
to the wider issue of the health of the participants. The
issues in respect of access to mental health services
are equally as applicable in respect of serious physical
illnesses. Whilst the crew may be given medical training,
there are some illnesses, such as the treatment of cancer,
which remain the purview of specialists. Asked in an
interview with *The Guardian* about what happens if a
crewmember becomes ill, Bas Lansdorp stated the exact
details are still to be determined. (15) Given that both the
mental and physical health of a small group are a crucial
aspect of the success of the mission, this lack of detail—a
feature that runs throughout the entire project—must
raise questions about the liability of parties on Earth for
injury caused to any of the crew.

The third, and broadest, issue in relation to the
ethics of the mission is the extent to which the Mars One
project has the right to establish a permanent settlement
on Mars. The Mars One website makes regular references
to the exploration of Columbus and Shackleton. Alluding to
these colonial ventures, designed to expand the resource
base of their respective empires, serves only to highlight
the irrevocable nature of the human settlement of Mars.
The Martian biosphere—if the planet does still support
life, a key unanswered scientific question—is unique and
largely free from human interference. A crewed base on
Mars would alter the distinct biological characteristics
of the environment. Human activity inevitably creates

waste, even with recycling; there will be a human impact upon this alien environment. While there may be compelling arguments as to why Mars is ideal for human settlement, there is no evidence that this Mars One project has received any independent, rigorous ethical scrutiny.

SETTLEMENT: THE COLONIAL LEGACY AND CUSTOMARY INTERNATIONAL LAW

Aside from the technical and ethical questions raised by Mars One, there are substantial legal and political questions that will have to be overcome. The colonial issue, mentioned above, of itself raises significant legal and political questions. The Netherlands and the United States, to the extent that Mars One incorporates and becomes subject to the jurisdiction of the United States, have less than spotless histories with regards to colonization. The first question to ask is whether Mars One could become a colony in the historical and legal sense.

A colony is [a] dependent political community, consisting of a number of citizens of the same country who have emigrated there from to people another, and remain subject to the mother country. It is a settlement in a foreign country possessed and cultivated, either wholly or partially, by immigrants and their descendants, who have a political connection with and subordination to the mother country, whence they emigrated. In other words, it is a place peopled from some more ancient city or country. (16)

At first blush, it may seem that that traditional legal and political concept of a colony does not apply simply because the potential colonists will come from several countries. In fact, the argument will likely be made by private space advocates that the "colonists" who come from several countries will not be colonists in the traditional sense because Mars One is a private venture and will be not be subject to the jurisdiction of any terrestrial government. However, the current body of international space law invalidates that belief. Specifically, Article VI of the Outer Space Treaty states:

> States Parties to the Treaty shall bear international responsibility for national activities in outer space, including the moon and other celestial bodies, whether such activities are carried on by governmental agencies *or by non-governmental entities*, and for assuring that national activities are carried out in conformity with the provisions set forth in the present Treaty. The activities of non-governmental entities in outer space, including the moon and other celestial bodies, shall require authorization and continuing supervision by the appropriate State Party to the Treaty. When activities are carried on in outer space, including the moon and other celestial bodies, by an international organization, responsibility for compliance with this Treaty shall be borne both by the international organization and by the States Parties to the Treaty participating in such organization.

This means that Mars One, as a non-governmental entity incorporated as a nonprofit in the Netherlands, is subject to the continuing jurisdiction of the Netherlands. Moreover, should Mars One incorporate as a nonprofit in the United States, it too would be subject to the continuing jurisdiction of the United States. (17) Mars One and its colonists would be considered non-governmental entities. They would remain under the jurisdiction of both the Netherlands and the United States government per Article VI, which in effect would make both nations their "mother country" and hence make the settlement a colony of both nations. (18) Since Mars One will be considered a colony of both the Netherlands and the United States, the next question is whether either country wishes to be burdened with the potential stigma of colonialism. The United States and the Netherlands in particular do not have a good history with colonialism, and a private venture that would create an extraterrestrial colony could be construed as a sovereign claim of territory that may be unpalatable in the realms of international law and politics.

In addition, the establishment of a Martian colony may have even greater legal effects. The Agreement Governing the Activities of States on the Moon and Other Celestial Bodies (the Moon Treaty) is considered to be a "failed treaty" because few nations have agreed to be bound by its provisions. One country that has ratified the treaty, however, is the Netherlands. This makes the precepts of the Moon Treaty legally binding upon a colonization effort by Mars One. Specifically, Article 7(1) dealing with the alteration of the environment and Article 11, which deals with resource development, would be pertinent and enforceable upon the Netherlands.

This could become problematic because the United States is not a party to this theaty. The Netherlands would have to ensure that Mars One was complying with the Moon Treaty, which means that the United States' acceptance of the Netherlands' adherence to the Moon Treaty could be construed as customary acceptance of the Moon

Treaty or, at the very least, the acceptance of an international standard of behavior in harmony with the Moon Treaty. The United States would have to expressly assert its rejection of the Moon Treaty and declare that it does not intend to be legally bound by customary law through its acquiescence to the Netherlands' performance of its international legal obligations under the Moon Treaty to avoid this issue.

TICKET TO RIDE? MARS ONE AND LAUNCH LICENSING

Complicit with the issue of colonialism is the issue of obtaining a launch license. The only practical way for Mars One to establish a colony on Mars is to perform its activities under the jurisdiction of the United States, which means Mars One would be subject to Title 51, Chapter 509, more commonly known as the Commercial Space Launch Act of 1984, and would be required to obtain a launch license. However, obtaining a launch license is no trivial matter, and more so with an endeavor like Mars One. If the United States issued a launch license to Mars One and the Netherlands gave its approval as well, that license would have to potentially cover decades of launch activities to not only start the colony, but also to resupply it and grow it. In other words, to the extent that the commitment of those who journey to Mars will be all in, the governments of the United States and the Netherlands would have to similarly commit all in when and if it grants a license for Mars One to proceed.

Any license granted to Mars One would have to be irrevocable and last in perpetuity because the survival of the colony would be wholly dependent on Mars One to resupply and grow the colony via launches from Earth. (19) A license that does not cover for the duration of mission would threaten the colonists' survival; i.e. the possibility that the launch license might be revoked or denied for future launches to support the colony could prove fatal for existing colonists on Mars because it would bring into question the ability to resupply and populate the colony. This fact alone will cause great hesitation because both governments would be, for all practical matters, diluting their ability under Article VI of the Outer Space Treaty to terminate the mission while being fully encumbered with the responsibility of its potential failure. In effect, such a license could not be morally revoked and could only expire in the event that the colony failed, at which point both governments could refuse to give their approval for any further adventures by Mars One.

A key issue here is whether either country is willing to allow such a high-risk venture to proceed. Mars One, as currently envisioned, has a high probability of failure, if not during the transit to Mars then during the initial settlement effort. The political, public, and media response to the death of the crew would be significant, especially if the public witnesses their demise on the proposed reality television program. The ensuing firestorm of negative media coverage, the public condemnation, the subsequent political backlash, and the inevitable geopolitical soft-power exploitation of the colony's demise will be significant and may very well sour the appetite for future government and/or private settlement efforts. This, along with the potential national security issues, the international and domestic legal questions, and the geopolitical questions that the colony would raise, suggests that Mars One would likely not receive the requisite launch license to not only start the project but to sustain it as well.

KEEP IT IN THE FAMILY? DOMESTIC ARRANGEMENTS AND MARS ONE

Another topic that is not brought up during the media excitement surrounding the proposed mission is the domestic/family legal issues that will arise as a result of the crew permanently leaving to start a new life on another planet, such as divorce. Many of the 100 selectees are married and have children. If the current and future selectees are married and go to Mars, what becomes of their spouses? In other words, will their spouses continue to be married to the settlers, or could they receive a divorce before the colonists leave or otherwise have their marriages annulled?

United States law, and the law of the particular state the colonists reside in before they depart, would likely control the issue. A divorce could likely be granted on no-fault grounds, since most jurisdictions in the United States recognize this type of divorce. However, the decision by one spouse to abandon his or her family to start a new life and, potentially, with a new spouse, is bound to create a divide and could result in a contentious divorce on fault grounds even during the preliminary selection process. However, as the mission draws closer, so will the reality that one spouse will be abandoning the other and, with it, the potential for conflict and the possibility of divorce proceedings on fault grounds. While some selectees may argue that they were going to give their spouse a divorce anyways, state laws concerning divorce may find that the spouse leaving for Mars may be liable for alimony or child support in the case of those selectees who may have minor children.

A court order mandating alimony or child support in one jurisdiction can be enforced in another state, which means that a state court could hold a selectee in contempt of court if he/she is scheduled to leave the planet, which potentially could be seen as disregarding his/her legal obligations under the court-ordered decree of divorce. Unless the selectee or Mars One creates a trust to pay for alimony and/or child support upon the selectee's departure, a state court could conceivably make an order forbidding the selectee to leave on the mission, which could be enforced by local law enforce-ment, and even result in confinement. The question then is whether Mars One would be able to take on the financial responsibility of alimony and child support obligations of its colonists and whether a state court would allow it to do so. In the grander scheme of the dream of Mars coloniza-tion, the reality of this basic family legal question must be answered along with other legal and political questions that will arise in the course of preparing for the mission.

CONCLUSION

Mars One is an ambitious undertaking and an inspiration to those who wish to see and participate in the expansion of humanity into the solar system. Yet this grand vision and promise of adventure does not negate the reality of the issues that must be recognized and addressed before that vision can be realized. Simply wishing the problems away and assuming that they can be sorted out before the first launch is not the foundation needed for the first human exploration to Mars.

Half a century of human space exploration has shown that the devil is in the details, and Mars One ignores those details at its peril. Unless the reality of the challenges facing Mars One are acknowledged and addressed by the leaders of this project, the current tide of positive media attention will turn on Mars One and leave those who believed in the vision created by its progenitors disillusioned and detriment future endeavors by private space to develop the solar system.

1. What is one of the most "crucial" difficulties of the Mars One project, according to the authors?

2. The authors state that a problem that is "every bit as deadly" to the Mars One crew as technical problems is the psychological issues that would affect the astronauts. What are some psychological problems that the crew might face?

CHAPTER 2

WHAT POLICY MAKERS SAY

Policies often seem to lag behind the times as technologies develop at a far greater speed than the political process.

Yet, when it comes to space travel and the exploration of other planets, this phenomenon seems to be reversed. The space race between the Soviet Union and the United States from the 1950s onward prompted international treaties that regulate human activities in space—activities that, even half a century later, remain dreams of the future. Humanity's efforts to explore and exploit other celestial bodies may not have kept up with earlier expectations, however, recent discoveries and declarations of intent from politicians as well as private entrepreneurs give the impression that we are on the verge of a new era.

Undoubtedly, humanity's foray into space will be challenging not only in regard to technology but also where politics and the application of law are concerned.

"TREATY ON PRINCIPLES GOVERNING THE ACTIVITIES OF STATES IN THE EXPLORATION AND USE OF OUTER SPACE, INCLUDING THE MOON AND OTHER CELESTIAL BODIES," FROM THE UNITED NATIONS, JANUARY 27, 1967

The States Parties to this Treaty,

Inspired by the great prospects opening up before mankind as a result of man's entry into outer space,

Recognizing the common interest of all mankind in the progress of the exploration and use of outer space for peaceful purposes,

Believing that the exploration and use of outer space should be carried on for the benefit of all peoples irrespective of the degree of their economic or scientific development,

Desiring to contribute to broad international cooperation in the scientific as well as the legal aspects of the exploration and use of outer space for peaceful purposes,

Believing that such cooperation will contribute to the development of mutual understanding and to the strengthening of friendly relations between States and peoples,

Recalling resolution 1962 (XVIII), entitled "Declaration of Legal Principles Governing the Activities of States in the Exploration and Use of Outer Space", which was adopted unanimously by the United Nations General Assembly on 13 December 1963,

Recalling resolution 1884 (XVIII), calling upon States to refrain from placing in orbit around the Earth any objects carrying nuclear weapons or any other kinds of weapons of mass destruction or from installing such weapons on celestial bodies, which was adopted unanimously by the United Nations General Assembly on 17 October 1963,

Taking account of United Nations General Assembly resolution 110 (II) of 3 November 1947, which condemned propaganda designed or likely to provoke or encourage any threat to the peace, breach of the peace or act of aggression, and considering that the aforementioned resolution is applicable to outer space,

Convinced that a Treaty on Principles Governing the Activities of States in the Exploration and Use of Outer Space, including the Moon and Other Celestial Bodies, will further the purposes and principles of the Charter of the United Nations,

Have agreed on the following:

Article I—The exploration and use of outer space, including the Moon and other celestial bodies, shall be carried out for the benefit and in the interests of all countries, irrespective of their degree of economic or scientific development, and shall be the province of all mankind.

Outer space, including the Moon and other celestial bodies, shall be free for exploration and use by all States without discrimination of any kind, on a basis of equality and in accordance with international law, and there shall be free access to all areas of celestial bodies.

There shall be freedom of scientific investigation in outer space, including the Moon and other celestial bodies, and States shall facilitate and encourage international cooperation in such investigation.

Article II—Outer space, including the Moon and other celestial bodies, is not subject to national appropriation by claim of sovereignty, by means of use or occupation, or by any other means.

Article III—States Parties to the Treaty shall carry on activities in the exploration and use of outer space, including the Moon and other celestial bodies, in accordance with international law, including the Charter of the United Nations, in the interest of maintaining international peace and security and promoting international cooperation and understanding.

Article IV—States Parties to the Treaty undertake not to place in orbit around the Earth any objects carrying nuclear weapons or any other kinds of weapons of mass destruction, install such weapons on celestial bodies, or station such weapons in outer space in any other manner.

The Moon and other celestial bodies shall be used by all States Parties to the Treaty exclusively for peaceful purposes. The establishment of military bases, installations and fortifications, the testing of any type of weapons and the conduct of military manoeuvres on celestial bodies shall be forbidden. The use of military personnel for scientific research or for any other peaceful purposes shall not be prohibited. The use of any equipment or facility necessary for peaceful exploration of the Moon and other celestial bodies shall also not be prohibited.

Article V—States Parties to the Treaty shall regard astronauts as envoys of mankind in outer space and shall render to them all possible assistance in the event of accident, distress, or emergency landing on the territory of another State Party or on the high seas. When astronauts make such a landing, they shall be safely and promptly returned to the State of registry of their space vehicle.

In carrying on activities in outer space and on celestial bodies, the astronauts of one State Party shall render all possible assistance to the astronauts of other States Parties.

States Parties to the Treaty shall immediately inform the other States Parties to the Treaty or the Secretary-General of the United Nations of any phenomena they discover in outer space, including the Moon and other celestial bodies, which could constitute a danger to the life or health of astronauts.

Article VI—States Parties to the Treaty shall bear international responsibility for national activities in outer space, including the Moon and other celestial bodies, whether such activities are carried on by governmental agencies or by non-governmental entities, and for assuring that national activities are carried out in conformity with the provisions set forth in the present Treaty. The activities of non-governmental entities in outer space, including the Moon and other celestial bodies, shall require authorization and continuing supervision by the appropriate State Party to the Treaty. When activities are carried on in outer space, including the Moon and other celestial bodies, by an international organization, responsibility for compliance with this Treaty shall be borne both by the international organization and by the States Parties to the Treaty participating in such organization.

Article VII—Each State Party to the Treaty that launches or procures the launching of an object into outer space, including the Moon and other celestial bodies, and each State Party from whose territory or facility an object is launched, is internationally liable for damage to another State Party to the Treaty or to its natural or juridical persons by such object or its component parts on the Earth, in air space or in outer space, including the Moon and other celestial bodies.

Article VIII—A State Party to the Treaty on whose registry an object launched into outer space is carried shall retain jurisdiction and control over such object, and over any personnel thereof, while in outer space or on a celestial body. Ownership of objects launched into outer space, including objects landed or constructed on a celestial body, and of their component parts, is not affected by their presence in outer space or on a celestial body or by their return to the Earth. Such objects or component parts found beyond the limits of the State Party to the Treaty on whose registry they are carried shall be returned to that State Party, which shall, upon request, furnish identifying data prior to their return.

Article IX—In the exploration and use of outer space, including the Moon and other celestial bodies, States Parties to the Treaty shall be guided by the principle of cooperation and mutual assistance and shall conduct all their activities in outer space, including the Moon and other celestial bodies, with due regard to the corresponding interests of all other States Parties to the Treaty. States Parties to the Treaty shall pursue studies of outer space, including the Moon and other celestial bodies, and conduct exploration of them so as to avoid their harmful contamination and also adverse changes in the environment of the Earth resulting from the introduction of extraterrestrial matter and, where necessary, shall adopt appropriate measures for this purpose. If a State

Party to the Treaty has reason to believe that an activity or experiment planned by it or its nationals in outer space, including the Moon and other celestial bodies, would cause potentially harmful interference with activities of other States Parties in the peaceful exploration and use of outer space, including the Moon and other celestial bodies, it shall undertake appropriate international consultations before proceeding with any such activity or experiment. A State Party to the Treaty which has reason to believe that an activity or experiment planned by another State Party in outer space, including the Moon and other celestial bodies, would cause potentially harmful interference with activities in the peaceful exploration and use of outer space, including the Moon and other celestial bodies, may request consultation concerning the activity or experiment.

Article X—In order to promote international cooperation in the exploration and use of outer space, including the Moon and other celestial bodies, in conformity with the purposes of this Treaty, the States Parties to the Treaty shall consider on a basis of equality any requests by other States Parties to the Treaty to be afforded an opportunity to observe the flight of space objects launched by those States.

The nature of such an opportunity for observation and the conditions under which it could be afforded shall be determined by agreement between the States concerned.

Article XI—In order to promote international cooperation in the peaceful exploration and use of outer space, States Parties to the Treaty conducting activities in outer space, including the Moon and other celestial bodies, agree to inform the Secretary-General of the United Nations as well as the public and the international scientific community, to the greatest extent feasible and practicable, of the nature, conduct, locations and results of such activities. On receiving the said information, the Secretary-General of the United Nations should be prepared to disseminate it immediately and effectively.

Article XII—All stations, installations, equipment and space vehicles on the Moon and other celestial bodies shall be open to representatives of other States Parties to the Treaty on a basis of reciprocity. Such representatives shall give reasonable advance notice of a projected visit, in order that appropriate consultations may be held and that maximum precautions may be taken to assure safety and to avoid interference with normal operations in the facility to be visited.

Article XIII—The provisions of this Treaty shall apply to the activities of States Parties to the Treaty in the exploration and use of outer space, including the Moon and other celestial bodies, whether such activities are carried on by a single State Party to the Treaty or jointly with other States, including cases where they are carried on within the framework of international intergovern-mental organizations.

Any practical questions arising in connection with activities carried on by international intergovernmental organizations in the exploration and use of outer space, including the Moon and other celestial bodies, shall be resolved by the States Parties to the Treaty either with the appropriate international organization or with one or more States members of that international organization, which are Parties to this Treaty.

Article XIV—1. This Treaty shall be open to all States for signature. Any State which does not sign this Treaty before its entry into force in accordance with paragraph 3 of this article may accede to it at any time.

2. This Treaty shall be subject to ratification by signatory States. Instruments of ratification and instruments of accession shall be deposited with the Governments of the Union of Soviet Socialist Republics, the United Kingdom of Great Britain and Northern Ireland and the United States of America, which are hereby designated the Depositary Governments.

3. This Treaty shall enter into force upon the deposit of instruments of ratification by five Governments including the Governments designated as Depositary Governments under this Treaty.

4. For States whose instruments of ratification or accession are deposited subsequent to the entry into force of this Treaty, it shall enter into force on the date of the deposit of their instruments of ratification or accession.

5. The Depositary Governments shall promptly inform all signatory and acceding States of the date of each signature, the date of deposit of each instrument of ratification of and accession to this Treaty, the date of its entry into force and other notices.

6. This Treaty shall be registered by the Depositary Governments pursuant to Article 102 of the Charter of the United Nations.

Article XV—Any State Party to the Treaty may propose amendments to this Treaty.

Amendments shall enter into force for each State Party to the Treaty accepting the amendments upon their acceptance by a majority of the States Parties to the Treaty and thereafter for each remaining State Party to the Treaty on the date of acceptance by it.

Article XVI—Any State Party to the Treaty may give notice of its withdrawal from the Treaty one year after its entry into force by written notification to the Depositary Governments. Such withdrawal shall take effect one year from the date of receipt of this notification.

Article XVII—This Treaty, of which the Chinese, English, French, Russian and Spanish texts are equally authentic, shall be deposited in the archives of the Depositary Governments. Duly certified copies of this Treaty shall be transmitted by the Depositary Governments to the Governments of the signatory and acceding States.

IN WITNESS WHEREOF the undersigned, duly authorized, have signed this Treaty.

DONE in triplicate, at the cities of London, Moscow and Washington, D.C., the twenty-seventh day of January, one thousand nine hundred and sixty-seven.

1. Do you think an international treaty written by humans is applicable in space?

2. Do you think this treaty was somewhat premature based on the technological advances of the time in which it was written?

"AGREEMENT GOVERNING THE ACTIVITIES OF STATES ON THE MOON AND OTHER CELESTIAL BODIES," FROM THE UNITED NATIONS, DECEMBER 18, 1979

The States Parties to this Agreement,

Noting the achievements of States in the exploration and use of the Moon and other celestial bodies,

Recognizing that the Moon, as a natural satellite of the Earth, has an important role to play in the exploration of outer space,

Determined to promote on the basis of equality the further development of cooperation among States in the exploration and use of the Moon and other celestial bodies,

Desiring to prevent the Moon from becoming an area of international conflict,

Bearing in mind the benefits which may be derived from the exploitation of the natural resources of the Moon and other celestial bodies,

Recalling the Treaty on Principles Governing the Activities of States in the Exploration and Use of Outer Space, including the Moon and Other Celestial Bodies, the Agreement on the Rescue of Astronauts, the Return of Astronauts and the Return of Objects Launched into Outer Space, the Convention on International Liability for Damage Caused by Space Objects,

and the Convention on Registration of Objects Launched into Outer Space,

Taking into account the need to define and develop the provisions of these international instruments in relation to the Moon and other celestial bodies, having regard to further progress in the exploration and use of outer space,

Have agreed on the following:

ARTICLE 1

1. The provisions of this Agreement relating to the Moon shall also apply to other celestial bodies within the solar system, other than the Earth, except insofar as specific legal norms enter into force with respect to any of these celestial bodies.

2. For the purposes of this Agreement reference to the Moon shall include orbits around or other trajectories to or around it.

3. This Agreement does not apply to extraterrestrial materials which reach the surface of the Earth by natural means.

ARTICLE 2

All activities on the Moon, including its exploration and use, shall be carried out in accordance with international law, in particular the Charter of the United Nations, and taking into account the Declaration on Principles of International Law concerning Friendly Relations and Cooperation among States in accordance with the Charter of the United Nations, adopted by the General Assembly on 24 October 1970, in the interest of maintaining international peace and security and promoting international cooperation and mutual understanding, and with due regard to the corresponding interests of all other States Parties.

ARTICLE 3

1. The Moon shall be used by all States Parties exclusively for peaceful purposes.

2. Any threat or use of force or any other hostile act or threat of hostile act on the Moon is prohibited. It is likewise prohibited to use the Moon in order to commit any such act or to engage in any such threat in relation to the Earth, the Moon, spacecraft, the personnel of spacecraft or man-made space objects.

3. States Parties shall not place in orbit around or other trajectory to or around the Moon objects carrying nuclear weapons or any other kinds of weapons of mass destruction or place or use such weapons on or in the Moon.

4. The establishment of military bases, installations and fortifications, the testing of any type of weapons and the conduct of military manoeuvres on the Moon shall be forbidden. The use of military personnel for scientific research or for any other peaceful purposes shall not be prohibited. The use of any equipment or facility necessary for peaceful exploration and use of the Moon shall also not be prohibited.

ARTICLE 4

1. The exploration and use of the Moon shall be the province of all mankind and shall be carried out

for the benefit and in the interests of all countries, irrespective of their degree of economic or scientific development. Due regard shall be paid to the interests of present and future generations as well as to the need to promote higher standards of living and conditions of economic and social progress and development in accordance with the Charter of the United Nations.

2. States Parties shall be guided by the principle of cooperation and mutual assistance in all their activities concerning the exploration and use of the Moon. International cooperation in pursuance of this Agreement should be as wide as possible and may take place on a multilateral basis, on a bilateral basis or through international intergovernmental organizations.

ARTICLE 5

1. States Parties shall inform the Secretary-General of the United Nations as well as the public and the international scientific community, to the greatest extent feasible and practicable, of their activities concerned with the exploration and use of the Moon. Information on the time, purposes, locations, orbital parameters and duration shall be given in respect of each mission to the Moon as soon as possible after launching, while information on the results of each mission, including scientific results, shall be furnished upon completion of the mission. In the case of a mission lasting more than sixty days, informa-

tion on conduct of the mission, including any scientific results, shall be given periodically, at thirty-day intervals. For missions lasting more than six months, only significant additions to such information need be reported thereafter.

2. If a State Party becomes aware that another State Party plans to operate simultaneously in the same area of or in the same orbit around or trajectory to or around the Moon, it shall promptly inform the other State of the timing of and plans for its own operations.

3. In carrying out activities under this Agreement, States Parties shall promptly inform the Secretary-General, as well as the public and the international scientific community, of any phenomena they discover in outer space, including the Moon, which could endanger human life or health, as well as of any indication of organic life.

ARTICLE 6

1. There shall be freedom of scientific investigation on the Moon by all States Parties without discrimination of any kind, on the basis of equality and in accordance with international law.

2. In carrying out scientific investigations and in furtherance of the provisions of this Agreement, the States Parties shall have the right to collect on and remove from the Moon samples of its mineral and other substances. Such samples shall remain at the disposal of those States Parties which caused them

to be collected and may be used by them for scientific purposes. States Parties shall have regard to the desirability of making a portion of such samples available to other interested States Parties and the international scientific community for scientific investigation. States Parties may in the course of scientific investigations also use mineral and other substances of the Moon in quantities appropriate for the support of their missions.

3. States Parties agree on the desirability of exchanging scientific and other personnel on expeditions to or installations on the Moon to the greatest extent feasible and practicable.

ARTICLE 7

1. In exploring and using the Moon, States Parties shall take measures to prevent the disruption of the existing balance of its environment, whether by introducing adverse changes in that environment, by its harmful contamination through the introduction of extra-environmental matter or otherwise. States Parties shall also take measures to avoid harmfully affecting the environment of the Earth through the introduction of extraterrestrial matter or otherwise.

2. States Parties shall inform the Secretary-General of the United Nations of the measures being adopted by them in accordance with paragraph 1 of this article and shall also, to the maximum extent feasible, notify him in advance of all placements by them of

radioactive materials on the Moon and of the purposes of such placements.

3. States Parties shall report to other States Parties and to the Secretary-General concerning areas of the Moon having special scientific interest in order that, without prejudice to the rights of other States Parties, consideration may be given to the designation of such areas as international scientific preserves for which special protective arrangements are to be agreed upon in consultation with the competent bodies of the United Nations.

ARTICLE 8

1. States Parties may pursue their activities in the exploration and use of the Moon anywhere on or below its surface, subject to the provisions of this Agreement.

2. For these purposes States Parties may, in particular:

   (a) Land their space objects on the Moon and launch them from the Moon;

   (b) Place their personnel, space vehicles, equipment, facilities, stations and installations anywhere on or below the surface of the Moon;

   Personnel, space vehicles, equipment, facilities, stations and installations may move or be moved freely over or below the surface of the Moon.

3. Activities of States Parties in accordance with paragraphs 1 and 2 of this article shall not interfere with the activities of other States Parties on the Moon. Where such interference may occur, the States Parties con-

cerned shall undertake consultations in accordance with article 15, paragraphs 2 and 3, of this Agreement.

ARTICLE 9

1. States Parties may establish manned and unmanned stations on the Moon. A State Party establishing a station shall use only that area which is required for the needs of the station and shall immediately inform the Secretary-General of the United Nations of the location and purposes of that station. Subsequently, at annual intervals that State shall likewise inform the Secretary-General whether the station continues in use and whether its purposes have changed.

2. Stations shall be installed in such a manner that they do not impede the free access to all areas of the Moon of personnel, vehicles and equipment of other States Parties conducting activities on the Moon in accordance with the provisions of this Agreement or of article I of the Treaty on Principles Governing the Activities of States in the Exploration and Use of Outer Space, including the Moon and Other Celestial Bodies.

ARTICLE 10

1. States Parties shall adopt all practicable measures to safeguard the life and health of persons on the Moon. For this purpose they shall regard any person on the Moon as an astronaut within the meaning of article V of the Treaty on Principles Governing

the Activities of States in the Exploration and Use of Outer Space, including the Moon and Other Celestial Bodies and as part of the personnel of a spacecraft within the meaning of the Agreement on the Rescue of Astronauts, the Return of Astronauts and the Return of Objects Launched into Outer Space.

2. States Parties shall offer shelter in their stations, installations, vehicles and other facilities to persons in distress on the Moon.

ARTICLE 11

1. The Moon and its natural resources are the common heritage of mankind, which finds its expression in the provisions of this Agreement, in particular in paragraph 5 of this article.

2. The Moon is not subject to national appropriation by any claim of sovereignty, by means of use or occupation, or by any other means.

3. Neither the surface nor the subsurface of the Moon, nor any part thereof or natural resources in place, shall become property of any State, international intergovernmental or non-governmental organization, national organization or non-governmental entity or of any natural person. The placement of personnel, space vehicles, equipment, facilities, stations and installations on or below the surface of the Moon, including structures connected with its surface or subsurface, shall not create a right of ownership over the surface or the subsurface of the Moon or any areas thereof. The foregoing provisions

are without prejudice to the international regime referred to in paragraph 5 of this article.

4. States Parties have the right to exploration and use of the Moon without discrimination of any kind, on the basis of equality and in accordance with international law and the terms of this Agreement.

5. States Parties to this Agreement hereby undertake to establish an international regime, including appropriate procedures, to govern the exploitation of the natural resources of the Moon as such exploitation is about to become feasible. This provision shall be implemented in accordance with article 18 of this Agreement.

6. In order to facilitate the establishment of the international regime referred to in paragraph 5 of this article, States Parties shall inform the Secretary-General of the United Nations as well as the public and the international scientific community, to the greatest extent feasible and practicable, of any natural resources they may discover on the Moon.

7. The main purposes of the international regime to be established shall include:

(a) The orderly and safe development of the natural resources of the Moon;

(b) The rational management of those resources;

(c) The expansion of opportunities in the use of those resources;

(d) An equitable sharing by all States Parties in the benefits derived from those resources, whereby the interests and needs of the developing countries, as well as the efforts of those countries which have contributed either directly or indirectly to the exploration of the Moon, shall be given special consideration.

8. All the activities with respect to the natural resources of the Moon shall be carried out in a manner compatible with the purposes specified in paragraph 7 of this article and the provisions of article 6, paragraph 2, of this Agreement.

ARTICLE 12

1. States Parties shall retain jurisdiction and control over their personnel, vehicles, equipment, facilities, stations and installations on the Moon. The ownership of space vehicles, equipment, facilities, stations and installations shall not be affected by their presence on the Moon.

2. Vehicles, installations and equipment or their component parts found in places other than their intended location shall be dealt with in accordance with article 5 of the Agreement on the Rescue of Astronauts, the Return of Astronauts and the Return of Objects Launched into Outer Space.

3. In the event of an emergency involving a threat to human life, States Parties may use the equipment, vehicles, installations, facilities or supplies of other States Parties on the Moon. Prompt notification of such use shall be made to the Secretary-General of the United Nations or the State Party concerned.

ARTICLE 13

A State Party which learns of the crash landing, forced landing or other unintended landing on the Moon of a space object, or its component parts, that were not launched by it, shall promptly inform the launching State Party and the Secretary-General of the United Nations.

ARTICLE 14

1. States Parties to this Agreement shall bear international responsibility for national activities on the Moon, whether such activities are carried on by governmental agencies or by non-governmental entities, and for assuring that national activities are carried out in conformity with the provisions set forth in this Agreement. States Parties shall ensure that non-governmental entities under their jurisdiction shall engage in activities on the Moon only under the authority and continuing supervision of the appropriate State Party.

2. States Parties recognize that detailed arrangements concerning liability for damage caused on the Moon, in addition to the provisions of the Treaty on Principles Governing the Activities of States in the Exploration and Use of Outer Space, including the Moon and Other Celestial Bodies and the Convention on International Liability for Damage Caused by Space Objects, may become necessary as a result of more extensive activities on the Moon. Any such arrangements shall

be elaborated in accordance with the procedure provided for in article 18 of this Agreement.

ARTICLE 15

1. Each State Party may assure itself that the activities of other States Parties in the exploration and use of the Moon are compatible with the provisions of this Agreement. To this end, all space vehicles, equipment, facilities, stations and installations on the Moon shall be open to other States Parties. Such States Parties shall give reasonable advance notice of a projected visit, in order that appropriate consultations may be held and that maximum precautions may be taken to assure safety and to avoid interference with normal operations in the facility to be visited. In pursuance of this article, any State Party may act on its own behalf or with the full or partial assistance of any other State Party or through appropriate international procedures within the framework of the United Nations and in accordance with the Charter.

2. A State Party which has reason to believe that another State Party is not fulfilling the obligations incumbent upon it pursuant to this Agreement or that another State Party is interfering with the rights which the former State has under this Agreement may request consultations with that State Party. A State Party receiving such a request shall enter into such consultations without delay. Any other State Party which requests to do so shall be entitled to take part in the

consultations. Each State Party participating in such consultations shall seek a mutually acceptable resolution of any controversy and shall bear in mind the rights and interests of all States Parties. The Secretary-General of the United Nations shall be informed of the results of the consultations and shall transmit the information received to all States Parties concerned.

3. If the consultations do not lead to a mutually acceptable settlement which has due regard for the rights and interests of all States Parties, the parties concerned shall take all measures to settle the dispute by other peaceful means of their choice appropriate to the circumstances and the nature of the dispute. If difficulties arise in connection with the opening of consultations or if consultations do not lead to a mutually acceptable settlement, any State Party may seek the assistance of the Secretary-General, without seeking the consent of any other State Party concerned, in order to resolve the controversy. A State Party which does not maintain diplomatic relations with another State Party concerned shall participate in such consultations, at its choice, either itself or through another State Party or the Secretary-General as intermediary.

ARTICLE 16

With the exception of articles 17 to 21, references in this Agreement to States shall be deemed to apply to any international intergovernmental organization which conducts space activities if the organization declares its acceptance of the rights and obligations provided for in this Agreement and if a majority of the States members of the organization are States Parties to this Agreement and to the Treaty on Principles Governing the Activities of States in the Exploration and Use of Outer Space, including the Moon and Other Celestial Bodies. States members of any such organization which are States Parties to this Agreement shall take all appropriate steps to ensure that the organization makes a declaration in accordance with the foregoing.

ARTICLE 17

Any State Party to this Agreement may propose amendments to the Agreement. Amendments shall enter into force for each State Party to the Agreement accepting the amendments upon their acceptance by a majority of the States Parties to the Agreement and thereafter for each remaining State Party to the Agreement on the date of acceptance by it.

ARTICLE 18

Ten years after the entry into force of this Agreement, the question of the review of the Agreement shall be included in the provisional agenda of the General Assembly of the United Nations in order to consider, in the light of past application of the Agreement, whether it requires revision. However, at any time after the Agreement has been in force for five years, the Secretary-General of the United Nations, as depositary, shall, at the request of one third of

the States Parties to the Agreement and with the concur-
rence of the majority of the States Parties, convene a conference of the States Parties to review this Agreement. A
review conference shall also consider the question of the
implementation of the provisions of article 11, paragraph
5, on the basis of the principle referred to in paragraph
1 of that article and taking into account in particular any
relevant technological developments.

ARTICLE 19

1. This Agreement shall be open for signature by all States
   at United Nations Headquarters in New York.

2. This Agreement shall be subject to ratification by signatory States. Any State which does not sign this Agreement before its entry into force in accordance with
   paragraph 3 of this article may accede to it at any time.
   Instruments of ratification or accession shall be deposited with the Secretary-General of the United Nations.

3. This Agreement shall enter into force on the thirtieth day
   following the date of deposit of the fifth instrument of
   ratification.

4. For each State depositing its instrument of ratification or
   accession after the entry into force of this Agreement,
   it shall enter into force on the thirtieth day following the
   date of deposit of any such instrument.

5. The Secretary-General shall promptly inform all signatory and acceding States of the date of each signature,
   the date of deposit of each instrument of ratification or
   accession to this Agreement, the date of its entry into
   force and other notices.

WHAT POLICY MAKERS SAY

ARTICLE 20

Any State Party to this Agreement may give notice of its withdrawal from the Agreement one year after its entry into force by written notification to the Secretary-General of the United Nations. Such withdrawal shall take effect one year from the date of receipt of this notification.

ARTICLE 21

The original of this Agreement, of which the Arabic, Chinese, English, French, Russian and Spanish texts are equally authentic, shall be deposited with the Secretary-General of the United Nations, who shall send certified copies thereof to all signatory and acceding States.

IN WITNESS WHEREOF the undersigned, being duly authorized thereto by their respective Governments, have signed this Agreement, opened for signature at New York on the eighteenth day of December, one thousand nine hundred and seventy-nine.

1. How does this expand on the previous treaty from 1967?

2. What rights, according to this treaty, do states or nations have on the Moon?

"REMARKS BY THE PRESIDENT ON SPACE EXPLORATION IN THE 21ST CENTURY," BY PRESIDENT BARACK OBAMA, FROM THE WHITE HOUSE, APRIL 15, 2010

THE PRESIDENT: Thank you, everybody. Thank you. (Applause.) Thank you so much. Thank you, everybody. Please have a seat. Thank you.

I want to thank Senator Bill Nelson and NASA Administrator Charlie Bolden for their extraordinary leadership. I want to recognize Dr. Buzz Aldrin as well, who's in the house. (Applause.) Four decades ago, Buzz became a legend. But in the four decades since he's also been one of America's leading visionaries and authorities on human space flight.

Few people -- present company excluded -- can claim the expertise of Buzz and Bill and Charlie when it comes to space exploration. I have to say that few people are as singularly unimpressed by Air Force One as those three. (Laughter.) Sure, it's comfortable, but it can't even reach low Earth orbit. And that obviously is in striking contrast to the Falcon 9 rocket we just saw on the launch pad, which will be tested for the very first time in the coming weeks.

A couple of other acknowledgments I want to make. We've got Congresswoman Sheila Jackson Lee from Texas visiting us, a big supporter of the space program. (Applause.) My director, Office of Science and Technology Policy -- in other words my chief science advisor -- John Holdren is here. (Applause.) And most of all I want to acknowledge your congresswoman Suzanne Kosmas, because every time I meet with her, including the flight down here, she reminds me of how important our NASA programs are and how important this facility is. And she is fighting for every single one of you and for her district and for the jobs in her district. And you should know that you've got a great champion in Congresswoman Kosmas. Please give her a big round of applause. (Applause.)

I also want to thank everybody for participating in today's conference. And gathered here are scientists, engineers, business leaders, public servants, and a few more astronauts as well. Last but not least, I want to thank the men and women of NASA for welcoming me to the Kennedy Space Center, and for your contributions not only to America, but to the world.

Here at the Kennedy Space Center we are surrounded by monuments and milestones of those contributions. It was from here that NASA launched the missions of Mercury and Gemini and Apollo. It was from here that Space Shuttle Discovery, piloted by Charlie Bolden, carried the Hubble Telescope into orbit, allowing us to plumb the deepest recesses of our galaxy. And I should point out, by the way, that in my private office just off the Oval, I've got the picture of Jupiter from the Hubble. So thank you, Charlie, for helping to decorate my office. (Laughter.) It was from here that men and women, propelled by sheer nerve and talent, set about pushing the boundaries of humanity's reach.

That's the story of NASA. And it's a story that started a little more than half a century ago, far from the Space Coast, in a remote and desolate region of what is now called Kazakhstan. Because it was from there that the

Soviet Union launched Sputnik, the first artificial satellite to orbit the Earth, which was little more than a few pieces of metal with a transmitter and a battery strapped to the top of a missile. But the world was stunned. Americans were dumbfounded. The Soviets, it was perceived, had taken the lead in a race for which we were not yet fully prepared.

But we caught up very quick. President Eisenhower signed legislation to create NASA and to invest in science and math education, from grade school to graduate school. In 1961, President Kennedy boldly declared before a joint session of Congress that the United States would send a man to the Moon and return him safely to the Earth within the decade. And as a nation, we set about meeting that goal, reaping rewards that have in the decades since touched every facet of our lives. NASA was at the forefront. Many gave their careers to the effort. And some have given far more.

In the years that have followed, the space race inspired a generation of scientists and innovators, including, I'm sure, many of you. It's contributed to immeasurable technological advances that have improved our health and well-being, from satellite navigation to water purification, from aerospace manufacturing to medical imaging. Although, I have to say, during a meeting right before I came out on stage somebody said, you know, it's more than just Tang -- and I had to point out I actually really like Tang. (Laughter.) I thought that was very cool.

And leading the world to space helped America achieve new heights of prosperity here on Earth, while demonstrating the power of a free and open society to harness the ingenuity of its people.

And on a personal note, I have been part of that generation so inspired by the space program. 1961 was the year of my birth -- the year that Kennedy made his announcement. And one of my earliest memories is sitting on my grandfather's shoulders, waving a flag as astronauts arrived in Hawaii. For me, the space program has always captured an essential part of what it means to be an American -- reaching for new heights, stretching beyond what previously did not seem possible. And so, as President, I believe that space exploration is not a luxury, it's not an afterthought in America's quest for a brighter future -- it is an essential part of that quest.

So today, I'd like to talk about the next chapter in this story. The challenges facing our space program are different, and our imperatives for this program are different, than in decades past. We're no longer racing against an adversary. We're no longer competing to achieve a singular goal like reaching the Moon. In fact, what was once a global competition has long since become a global collaboration. But while the measure of our achievements has changed a great deal over the past 50 years, what we do -- or fail to do -- in seeking new frontiers is no less consequential for our future in space and here on Earth.

So let me start by being extremely clear: I am 100 percent committed to the mission of NASA and its future. (Applause.) Because broadening our capabilities in space will continue to serve our society in ways that we can scarcely imagine. Because exploration will once more inspire wonder in a new generation -- sparking passions and launching careers. And because, ultimately, if we fail to press forward in the pursuit of discovery, we are ceding our future and we are ceding that essential element of the American character.

I know there have been a number of questions raised about my administration's plan for space exploration, especially in this part of Florida where so many rely on NASA as a source of income as well as a source of pride and community. And these questions come at a time of transition, as the space shuttle nears its scheduled retirement after almost 30 years of service. And understandably, this adds to the worries of folks concerned not only about their own futures but about the future of the space program to which they've devoted their lives.

But I also know that underlying these concerns is a deeper worry, one that precedes not only this plan but this administration. It stems from the sense that people in Washington -- driven sometimes less by vision than by politics -- have for years neglected NASA's mission and undermined the work of the professionals who fulfill it. We've seen that in the NASA budget, which has risen and fallen with the political winds.

But we can also see it in other ways: in the reluctance of those who hold office to set clear, achievable objectives; to provide the resources to meet those objectives; and to justify not just these plans but the larger purpose of space exploration in the 21st century.

All that has to change. And with the strategy I'm outlining today, it will. We start by increasing NASA's budget by $6 billion over the next five years, even -- (applause) -- I want people to understand the context of this. This is happening even as we have instituted a freeze on discretionary spending and sought to make cuts elsewhere in the budget.

So NASA, from the start, several months ago when I issued my budget, was one of the areas where we didn't just maintain a freeze but we actually increased funding by $6 billion. By doing that we will ramp up robotic exploration of the solar system, including a probe of the Sun's atmosphere; new scouting missions to Mars and other destinations; and an advanced telescope to follow Hubble, allowing us to peer deeper into the universe than ever before.

We will increase Earth-based observation to improve our understanding of our climate and our world -- science that will garner tangible benefits, helping us to protect our environment for future generations.

And we will extend the life of the International Space Station likely by more than five years, while actually using it for its intended purpose: conducting advanced research that can help improve the daily lives of people here on Earth, as well as testing and improving upon our capabilities in space. This includes technologies like more efficient life support systems that will help reduce the cost of future missions. And in order to reach the space station, we will work with a growing array of private companies competing to make getting to space easier and more affordable. (Applause.)

Now, I recognize that some have said it is unfeasible or unwise to work with the private sector in this way. I disagree. The truth is, NASA has always relied on private industry to help design and build the vehicles that carry astronauts to space, from the Mercury capsule that carried John Glenn into orbit nearly 50 years ago, to the space shuttle Discovery currently orbiting overhead. By buying the services of space transportation -- rather than the vehicles themselves -- we can continue to ensure rigorous safety standards are met. But we will also accelerate the pace of innovations as companies -- from young startups to established leaders -- compete to design and build and launch new means of carrying people and materials out of our atmosphere.

In addition, as part of this effort, we will build on the good work already done on the Orion crew capsule. I've directed Charlie Bolden to immediately begin developing a rescue vehicle using this technology, so we are not forced to rely on foreign providers if it becomes necessary to quickly bring our people home from the International Space Station. And this Orion effort will be part of the technological foundation for advanced spacecraft to be used in future deep space missions. In fact, Orion will be readied for flight right here in this room. (Applause.)

Next, we will invest more than $3 billion to conduct research on an advanced "heavy lift rocket" -- a vehicle to efficiently send into orbit the crew capsules, propulsion systems, and large quantities of supplies needed to reach deep space. In developing this new vehicle, we will not only look at revising or modifying older models; we want to look at new designs, new materials, new technologies that will transform not just where we can go but what we can do when we get there. And we will finalize a rocket design no later than 2015 and then begin to build it. (Applause.) And I want everybody to understand: That's at least two years earlier than previously planned -- and that's conservative, given that the previous program was behind schedule and over budget.

At the same time, after decades of neglect, we will increase investment -- right away -- in other groundbreaking technologies that will allow astronauts to reach space sooner and more often, to travel farther and faster for less cost, and to live and work in space for longer periods of time more safely. That means tackling major scientific and technological challenges. How do we shield astronauts from radiation on longer missions? How do we harness resources on distant worlds? How do we supply spacecraft with energy needed for these far-reaching journeys? These are questions that we can answer and will answer. And these are the questions whose answers no doubt will reap untold benefits right here on Earth.

So the point is what we're looking for is not just to continue on the same path -- we want to leap into the future; we want major breakthroughs; a transformative agenda for NASA. (Applause.)

Now, yes, pursuing this new strategy will require that we revise the old strategy. In part, this is because the old strategy -- including the Constellation program -- was not fulfilling its promise in many ways. That's not just my assessment; that's also the assessment of a panel of respected non-partisan experts charged with looking at these issues closely. Now, despite this, some have had harsh words for the decisions we've made, including some individuals who I've got enormous respect and admiration for.

But what I hope is, is that everybody will take a look at what we are planning, consider the details of what we've laid out, and see the merits as I've described them. The bottom line is nobody is more committed to manned space flight, to human exploration of space than I am. (Applause.) But we've got to do it in a smart way, and we can't just keep on doing the same old things that we've been doing and thinking that somehow is going to get us to where we want to go.

Some have said, for instance, that this plan gives up our leadership in space by failing to produce plans within NASA to reach low Earth orbit, instead of relying on companies and other countries. But we will actually reach space faster and more often under this new plan, in ways that will help us improve our technological capacity and lower our costs, which are both essential for the long-term sustainability of space flight. In fact, through our plan, we'll be sending many more astronauts to space over the next decade. (Applause.)

There are also those who criticized our decision to end parts of Constellation as one that will hinder space exploration below [sic] low Earth orbit. But it's precisely by investing in groundbreaking research and innovative companies that we will have the potential to rapidly trans- form our capabilities -- even as we build on the important work already completed, through projects like Orion, for future missions. And unlike the previous program, we are setting a course with specific and achievable milestones.

Early in the next decade, a set of crewed flights will test and prove the systems required for exploration beyond low Earth orbit. (Applause.) And by 2025, we expect new spacecraft designed for long journeys to allow us to begin the first-ever crewed missions beyond the Moon into deep space. (Applause.) So we'll start -- we'll start by sending astronauts to an asteroid for the first time in history. (Applause.) By the mid-2030s, I believe we can send humans to orbit Mars and return them safely to Earth. And a landing on Mars will follow. And I expect to be around to see it. (Applause.)

But I want to repeat -- I want to repeat this: Critical to deep space exploration will be the development of breakthrough propulsion systems and other advanced technologies. So I'm challenging NASA to break through these barriers. And we'll give you the resources to break through these barriers. And I know you will, with ingenuity and intensity, because that's what you've always done. (Applause.)

Now, I understand that some believe that we should attempt a return to the surface of the Moon first, as previously planned. But I just have to say pretty bluntly here: We've been there before. Buzz has been there. There's a lot more of space to explore, and a lot more to learn when we do. So I believe it's more important to ramp up our capabilities to reach -- and operate at -- a series of increasingly demanding targets, while advancing our technological capabilities with each step forward. And that's what this strategy does. And that's how we will ensure that our leadership in space is even stronger in this new century than it was in the last. (Applause.)

Finally, I want to say a few words about jobs. Suzanne pointed out to me that the last time I was here, I made a very clear promise that I would help in the transition into a new program to make sure that people who are already going through a tough time here in this region were helped. And despite some reports to the contrary, my plan will add more than 2,500 jobs along the Space Coast in the next two years compared to the plan under the previous administration. So I want to make that point. (Applause.)

We're going to modernize the Kennedy Space Center, creating jobs as we upgrade launch facilities.

And there's potential for even more jobs as companies in Florida and across America compete to be part of a new space transportation industry. And some of those industry leaders are here today. This holds the promise of generating more than 10,000 jobs nationwide over the next few years. And many of these jobs will be created right here in Florida because this is an area primed to lead in this competition.

Now, it's true -- there are Floridians who will see their work on the shuttle end as the program winds down. This is based on a decision that was made six years ago, not six months ago, but that doesn't make it any less painful for families and communities affected as this decision becomes reality.

So I'm proposing -- in part because of strong lobbying by Bill and by Suzanne, as well as Charlie -- I'm proposing a $40 million initiative led by a high-level team from the White House, NASA, and other agencies to develop a plan for regional economic growth and job creation. And I expect this plan to reach my desk by August 15th. (Applause.) It's an effort that will help prepare this already skilled workforce for new opportunities in the space industry and beyond.

So this is the next chapter that we can write together here at NASA. We will partner with industry. We will invest in cutting-edge research and technology. We will set far-reaching milestones and provide the resources to reach those milestones. And step by step, we will push the boundaries not only of where we can go but what we can do.

Fifty years after the creation of NASA, our goal is no longer just a destination to reach. Our goal is the capacity for people to work and learn and operate and live safely beyond the Earth for extended periods of time, ultimately in ways that are more sustainable and even indefinite. And in fulfilling this task, we will not only extend humanity's reach in space -- we will strengthen America's leadership here on Earth.

Now, I'll close by saying this. I know that some Americans have asked a question that's particularly apt on Tax Day: Why spend money on NASA at all? Why spend money solving problems in space when we don't lack for problems to solve here on the ground? And obviously our country is still reeling from the worst economic turmoil we've known in generations. We have massive structural deficits that have to be closed in the coming years.

But you and I know this is a false choice. We have to fix our economy. We need to close our deficits. But for pennies on the dollar, the space program has fueled jobs and entire industries. For pennies on the dollar, the space program has improved our lives, advanced our society, strengthened our economy, and inspired generations of Americans. And I have no doubt that NASA can continue to fulfill this role. (Applause.) But that is why -- but I want to say clearly to those of you who work for NASA, but to the entire community that has been so supportive of the space program in this area: That is exactly why it's so essential that we pursue a new course and that we revitalize NASA and its mission -- not just with dollars, but with clear aims and a larger purpose.

Now, little more than 40 years ago, astronauts descended the nine-rung ladder of the lunar module called Eagle, and allowed their feet to touch the dusty surface of the Earth's only Moon. This was the culmination of a daring and perilous gambit -- of an endeavor that pushed the boundaries of our knowledge, of our technological prowess, of our very capacity as human beings to solve problems. It wasn't just the greatest achievement in NASA's history -- it was one of the greatest achievements in human history.

And the question for us now is whether that was the beginning of something or the end of something. I choose to believe it was only the beginning.

So thank you. God bless you. And may God bless the United States of America. Thank you. (Applause.)

1. What role does the space program play in American politics?

2. Which, of President Obama's outlined initiatives here, might garner the most support from the American public?

CHAPTER 3

WHAT ADVOCATES AND ADVOCACY ORGANIZATIONS SAY

O bviously, there is no human life on other planets yet, but there are various advocacy organizations campaigning for getting it there. Considering the enormous costs associated with manned spaceflight, organizations advocating astronautics probably have a harder time effecting progress than organizations championing social change on Earth. Astronautic organizations can't simply start small in their own neighborhood, and procuring a functioning spacecraft is considerably more difficult than setting up a local support group or advice center. What they can do, however, is provide information to the public at large, awaken people's interest, and contribute ideas to support their cause, possibly offering perspectives others have not considered before.

Advocacy groups such as Icarus Interstellar and The Space Settlement Institute, represented here, have dedicated a lot of thought, effort, and money into making space settlement a possibility in our lifetime. However, they approach the issue from different angles in this chapter, from a practical scientific exploration to a corporate call for private enterprise in space. The final excerpt deals with the more social difficulties of space colonization from the perspective of a space advocate and well-known space explorer: Buzz Aldrin.

"INTERSTELLAR COMPARISONS," BY ADAM CROWL, FROM ICARUS INTERSTELLAR, OCTOBER 1, 2014

Travelling to the stars within a human lifetime via the known laws of physics requires energies millions of times more potent than a trip to Mars, for example. In our energy hungry modern world the prospect seems fanciful, yet we are surrounded by energies and forces of comparable scale. By taming those forces we will be able to launch forth towards the stars and save our civilization and our biosphere.

How so? Consider the sunlight received every second by planet Earth, from the Sun. About 1.4 kilowatts of energy for every square metre directly facing the Sun – all 125 trillion of them. A total power supply of 175,000 trillion watts (175 petawatts), which is about 8,750 times more than the mere 20 terawatts human beings presently use. Earth receives a tiny fraction of the total – the Sun radiates about 2.2 billion times more, a colossal 385 trillion trillion watts (385 yottawatts).

Just how much does a starship need?

Project Daedalus proposed a fusion propelled star-probe able to fly to nearby stars in 50 years. To do so it would fuse 50,000 tonnes of deuterium and helium-3, expelling them as a rocket exhaust with an effective jet speed of 10,000 km/s. A total useful energy of 2500 million trillion joules (2.5 zettajoules) – the actual fusion energy available in the fuel was about 10 times this, due to the inefficiency of the fusion rocket motor. However that gives us a useful benchmark. This is dwarfed by the energy from the Sun. A full Daedalus fuel-tank is equivalent to about 4 hours of Sunlight received by planet Earth.

Another design, the laser-sail, masses 2,500 metric tons and requires a laser power of 5 petawatts, which accelerates the laser-sail starship 1 gee for 190 days to achieve a cruise speed of half light-speed or 150,000 km/s. A laser-power equal to what Earth intercepts from the Sun, 175 petawatts, could launch ~67 laser-sail starships per year. Total energy required is 8.24 yottajoules, per sail, is equal to 5.45 days of Earth-sunlight.

What else could the power to launch starships allow humankind to do? Power on the scale of worlds allows the remaking of worlds. Terraforming is the shaping of the dead worlds of the Solar System into more life-friendly environments. Mars, for example, is considered to be the most life-friendly planet other than Earth, yet it lacks an oxygen atmosphere, a significant magnetic field, and is colder than Antarctica. To release Earth-levels of oxygen from its rocks, power an artificial magnetosphere to deflect away the potentially harmful solar-wind, add nitrogen to reduce the fire risk, and keep the planet warm, the energies required are similar to those required to launch starships.

Releasing oxygen from Martian rocks requires melting the rock, usually composed of about 30% oxygen, and breaking the chemical bonds. What results is a melt of mixed metals, like iron, and semi-metals, like silicon, and oxygen gas, plus hardy compounds like aluminum oxide. For every kilogram of oxygen released, about 30 megajoules of energy are needed. Earth-normal oxygen levels require a partial pressure of 20 kilopascals (20 kPa), which means a mass of 5.4 tons of oxygen for every square metre of Martian surface – 775 trillion tons in total. The total energy required is 10 yottajoules. Adding 80 kPa of nitrogen, like Earth's atmosphere, requires mining the frozen nitrogen of Neptune's moon Triton, doubling the total energy required. Shipping it from Saturn's moon, Titan, as Kim Stanley Robinson imagines in his "Mars Trilogy", requires 8 times that energy, due Saturn's less favourable gravity conditions. Warming Mars to Earth-like levels, via collecting more solar energy with a vast solar mirror array, means collecting and directing about 50 petawatts of solar energy (equal to about 10 laser-sail starships). Before we use that energy to gently warm Mars, it can be concentrated via a "lens" into a solar-torch able to burn oxygen out of Mars's rocks. With 50 petawatts of useful energy the lens can liberate sufficient oxygen for breathing in a bit over 6 years.

The final task, creating an artificial magnetosphere, is puny by comparison. A superconducting magnetic loop, wrapped around the Martian equator, can be used, powered up to a magnetic field energy of ~620,000 trillion joules (620 petajoules), by about 12.4 seconds of energy from the solar-mirrors. This is sufficient to create a magnetosphere about 8 times the size of Mars, much like Earth's.

Total one-time energy budget is 20 yottajoules – 8,000 "Daedalus" starprobes, or 243 laser-sail starships equivalent. The ongoing power-supply of 50 petawatts is enough to propel 10 laser-sail starships at a time.

To terraform the other suitable planets and moons of the Solar System requires similar energy and power levels. For example, if we used a solar-torch to break up the surface ice of Jupiter's moon, Europa, into hydrogen and oxygen, then used it to 'encourage' the excess hydrogen to escape into space, the total energy would be about 8 yottajoules, surprisingly similar to what Mars requires. The nitrogen delivery cost is about 6 yottajoules, again similar to Mars. Ongoing energy supply would be 10 petawatts – two starships worth.

A less exotic location to terraform would be the Moon. As well as proximity, it requires no extra input of energy from the Sun to stay warm. However, unlike Europa or Mars, water as well as atmosphere would need to be delivered, multiplying the energy required. If shallow seas are sufficient – an average of 100 metres of water over the whole surface – then the energy to deliver ice and nitrogen from Triton, then make oxygen from lunar rocks, is 27 yottajoules.

None of the worlds considered so far have Earth-like gravity – the only solid planet with close to Earth gravity is Venus. To remake Venus is a vastly more challenging task, as it has three main features that make it un-Earthly: too much atmosphere, too much day-time and not enough water. Take away the atmosphere and the planet would cool rapidly, so while it is often likened to Hell, the comparison is temporary. The energy required to remove 1 kilogram from Venus to infinity is 53.7 megajoules. Venus has over a thousand tons of atmosphere for every square metre of surface – some 467,000 trillion tons of which is carbon dioxide. To remove it all requires 25,600 yottajoules, thus removal is far from being an economical option, even in that future age when yottajoule energy budgets are commonplace.

One option is to freeze the atmosphere by shading the planet totally. To do so would require placing a vast shade in an orbit between Venus and the Sun, but about a million kilometres closer. In this position, or slightly closer, the gravity of the Sun and Venus are balanced, thus allowing the shade to stay fixed in the sky of Venus. With a width about twice Venus's 12,100 kilometres, the shade would allow Venus to cool down, over a period of decades. Eventually the carbon dioxide would rain, then snow, covering the planet in dry-ice. Some form of insulation would then be spread over the carbon dioxide to keep it from bursting forth as gas again. Alternatively it might be pumped into natural cavities, once the sub-surface of Venus is better mapped. The energy cost of assembling such a vast shade, which would mass thousands of tonnes at least, would be far less than the cost of removing the carbon dioxide. So close to the Sun, the shade would intercept the equivalent of 8 times what Earth receives from the Sun – 1,400 petawatts in total, sufficient to propel 280 laser-sail starships, or power the terraforming of the other planets. Or both.

The next desirable for Venus is the addition of water. If 100 metres depth is required, then the total energy to ship from Triton, is 144 yottajoules. Using 50 petawatts of power, the time to export is about 122 years, with a 30 year travel time for ice falling Sunwards from Neptune. The total energy of creating an artificial magnetosphere, similar in size to Earth's, would be 6 exajoules (6 million trillion joules) – a tiny fraction of the energy budget.

Further afield than the Inner System, or even the Outer Planets, is the Oort Cloud, a spherical swarm of comets thousand to ten thousand times the Earth-Sun distance. According to current theories of how the planets formed, there were thousands of objects, ranging in size from Pluto to Earth's Moon, which formed from the primordial disk of gas and dust surrounding the infant Sun. Most of these collided and coalesced to form the cores of the planets, but a significant fraction would have been slung into distant orbits, far from the Sun. According to one estimate, by astronomer Louis Strigari and colleagues, there are 100,000 such objects for every star.

The technology to send a laser beam to a starship accelerating to half light-speed over thousands of Earth-Sun distances opens up that vast new territory we're only just beginning to discover. For example, if a laser is able to send 5 petawatts to a laser-sail at 1,000 times the Earth-Sun distance, would be able to warm a Pluto-sized planet to Earth-like temperatures at a distance of a light-year.

In conclusion, the ability to power starships will allow the spread of the Earth's biosphere to thousands of worlds which would otherwise remain lifeless. Life on Earth spread out in abundance, aeons ago, once it learnt the trick of harnessing the Sun's energy via photosynthesis to make food from lifeless chemicals. Humankind can do the same, on a vastly greater scale — *it's the natural thing to do.*

1. How much energy is necessary for human life to be established on other planets?

2. What do you think about the author's conclusion—especially given the seemingly insurmountable obstacles scientists face in colonizing other planets?

"SPACE LAND CLAIMS RECOGNITION: *LEVERAGING THE INHERENT VALUE OF LUNAR LAND FOR BILLIONS IN PRIVATE SECTOR INVESTMENT,*" BY DOUGLAS O. JOBES AND ALAN B. WASSER, FROM THE SPACE SETTLEMENT INSTITUTE, AUGUST 9, 2004

International law bans governments from owning land on the Moon, but private entities could legally own such land. The possibility of acquiring a vast tract of undeveloped Lunar real estate would create a major incentive for the private sector to invest billions to independently finance and develop a regular space transportation system and permanent base on the Moon. Freeing the development of a Lunar transport system and base from dependence on government funding would not only provide significant taxpayer relief but would also help make the President's Moon-to-Mars proposal more sustainable.

To create a framework for the incentive, Congress should pass "land claims recognition" legislation legalizing private claims of land in space. A land claims recognition bill would not violate the ban on sovereign ownership if the "use and occupation" standard from civil law (rather than "gift of the sovereign" from common law) were used as the legal basis for the private claim.

Land claims recognition legislation would allow the U.S. government to "recognize" - acquiesce to, or decide not to contest - a private entity's claim to a large tract of Lunar land once the entity, using its own financial resources, successfully implemented a space transportation system and permanent Lunar base. The private entity, taking ownership of the land, could immediately sell or mortgage large portions of the claim to recoup their investment and generate a huge profit.

Note: A proposed draft version of space land claims recognition legislation is available for review at www.spacesettlement.org/law.

I. LEGALITY OF SPACE LAND CLAIMS LEGISLATION

Establishing the legality of land claims recognition legislation involves three considerations:
- Current space treaties
- Legal framework
- International obligations

CURRENT SPACE TREATIES

Land claims in space are addressed by the 1967 Outer Space Treaty and the 1979 Moon Treaty. The Outer Space Treaty, to which the U.S. and most other space-faring nations are signatories, in Article II sets restrictions on national ownership of property in space:

> Outer space, including the moon and other celestial bodies, is not subject to national appropriation by claim of sovereignty, by means of use or occupation, or by any other means.

Some argue that this provision also bans private ownership of land in space. Simply arranging Article II in bulleted list format shows the restriction was plainly meant only for nations, however:

Outer space, including the moon and other celestial bodies, is not subject to *national appropriation*

- by claim of sovereignty,
- by means of use or occupation, or
- by any other means

From the September 15, 1959 New York Times article "Pleas Are Expected to Mount For U.N. Control of Outer Space":

Secretary General Dag Hammarskjold, in the introduction to his annual report last year, urged "agreement on a basic rule that outer space and the celestial bodies therein are not considered *as capable of appropriation to any state.*"

The very existence of the 1979 Moon Treaty is evidence the 1967 Outer Space Treaty was never intended to legislate private land claims in space. The Moon Treaty does specifically attempt to ban private property in space. If the Outer Space Treaty, which was signed and ratified by many nations, had already banned private property in space, why the need for an entirely new treaty in 1979?

The U.S. never ratified the Moon Treaty. The treaty is generally regarded as a dead letter and is not binding on the U.S. or its citizens. That the U.S. refused to sign the Moon Treaty strongly indicates Congress never intended property rights to be placed in jeopardy by either treaty.

LEGAL FRAMEWORK

The appropriate legal framework for land claims recognition in space is the "use and occupation" standard from civil law. Use and occupation means the claimants, by establishing a permanent presence on the land, have mixed their labor with the soil and created property rights that are independent of government.

In civil law countries like France, property rights have never been based on sovereignty as they have in the U.S. (which inherited the "common law" standard from the U.K.). Even in the U.S, derivatives of civil law are used by some states. From the New American Encyclopedia:

> Common law was generally adopted in the U.S., although Louisiana state law is based upon the Code Napoleon, and other states have partially codified systems. Civil law often relies on precedent, just as many common law rules are codified by statute [as in civil law] for convenience.

Use and occupation must be the standard for any land claims regimen in space, because the common law standard cannot be applied on a Moon where sovereignty itself is barred by international treaty. Congress will have to decree that, because there can be no government on the Moon, a permanent base or settlement can give itself title just as though it were a government. Property deeds for land under its control will be recognized by U.S. courts of law, subject to specified limitations - just as titles issued by France, China, and even Iran are recognized by U.S. courts.

INTERNATIONAL OBLIGATIONS

The Outer Space Treaty makes it clear that opening the space frontier must "benefit all mankind" and that open access to all areas of celestial bodies must be provided.

> The exploration and use of outer space, including the moon and other celestial bodies, shall be carried out for the benefit and in the interest of all countries...and shall be the province of all mankind...and there shall be free access to all areas of celestial bodies.

Establishing a space line and permanent base open to all paying passengers regardless of nationality would certainly benefit all mankind, thus making it both necessary and sufficient to meet that very important condition of international law.

Participation by other space-faring nations would also help demonstrate these activities are in compliance with the "benefit of all mankind" requirement. Land claims recognition legislation could even direct the U.S. State Department to negotiate treaties requiring the private entities to form multinational consortia, to assure other nations that land claims recognition is not just an American attempt at a Lunar land grab.

II. VALUE OF LUNAR LAND

Space land claims recognition would turn land on the Moon and other celestial bodies into a vast source of wealth. That real estate will acquire enormous value after there is a permanent base or settlement, regular commercial access, and a system of property rights.

Governments have often used offers of land to draw settlers to new and hostile regions. Traditional land grants cannot be used as an incentive because sovereignty on the Moon is prohibited, but land claims recognition would have the same effect. The objective of land claims recognition in space is the use of property rights as an incentive *to motivate private individuals to do something of great value for the whole society.*

PROFITABILITY OF LAND IN A CLAIM

Lunar land will be offered for sale after months of worldwide press coverage produced by the race to be the first to settle the Moon. There will be land buyers with business purposes for buying and using the land, but there will be a much bigger speculative and investment market. Many people who will never leave Earth will buy Lunar land.

To help generate investment capital, should private entities be allowed to make a land claim after merely *committing* to build the space line and Moon base? No, because the dollar value of a Lunar land claim will only become high enough to be extremely profitable when people can actually go there, and speculators and investors know this. So Lunar land deeds recognized by the U.S. should be offered for sale only after the land is actually accessible - that is, when there is a transport system going back and forth often enough to support a permanent base. It will finally be understood to be land in the sky, not pie in the sky.

VALUE OF LAND ON THE MOON

How much is the real estate on the Moon worth? There are about 10 billion acres of land on the Moon. Assuming an average value of only $20 per acre, the total value of the land on the Moon would be:

10,000,000,000 acres x $20 per acre = $200,000,000,000 = *$200 billion*

Consultation with real estate professionals reveals that for deeds to Lunar property recognized by the U.S. government, $100 per acre is a more realistic but very conservative minimum. At $100 per acre, the value of land on the Moon becomes $1,000,000,000,000 - a *trillion* dollars.

Can there be any doubt that such huge sums would not act as a strong incentive for the private sector to risk financing and developing a space transportation system and Moon base?

HOPE'S EXPERIMENT WITH LUNAR LAND VALUE

In 1980, Mr. Dennis Hope "claimed" the Moon and started a business selling Lunar land "deeds." Thanks to Mr.

Hope, the average value of Lunar land, even on the most remote regions of the Moon's surface, is now known to be *at least* $20 per acre – even with the land undeveloped and completely inaccessible.

Since Mr. Hope's claim is not recognized by any court, he is in effect selling the deeds as novelty items. As startling as it may be, Mr. Hope has sold over two million of these deeds since 1980, according to his website www. lunarembassy.com. The asking price for one acre of Lunar land, as of June 2004, is $19.99. If two million buyers have been willing to purchase novelty deeds with no real or intrinsic value, consider the enormous demand among land investors, land speculators, and the general public if Lunar land deeds legally recognized by the U.S. government were offered for sale.

Dr. Jeffrey D. Fisher, a nationally recognized real estate expert, believes the sales of Mr. Hope's novelty deeds represents a fair comparable with the real Lunar deeds that may one day exist:

> One way appraisers estimate value is the comparable sales approach. That Mr. Hope has been able to sell novelty deeds for Lunar land at this price [$20 per acre] may be an indication of the actual novelty value per acre. If an entity were selling land sanctioned by the U.S. government, which would make the ownership rights more official, then I can see the value being even greater.

Dr. Fisher is the Director of the Center for Real Estate Studies at the Indiana University School of Business and Professor of Finance and Real Estate. Among his many publications relating to the science of property valuation, Dr. Fisher is co-author of "Real Estate Finance and Investments" (2005), "Income Property Valuation" (2003), and "Income Property Appraisal" (1994). With such a prominent real estate valuation expert acknowledging that a minimum value for Lunar land, based on novelty value, has reasonably been demonstrated - and further suggesting that government-sanctioned deeds would fetch an even higher price - there can be little doubt of the intrinsic value of Lunar land.

AMOUNT OF LAND RECOGNIZED

How large a claim the U.S. should recognize would be up to Congress to decide. For example, the U.S. might decide to recognize a claim of no more than 4% of the Moon's surface - about 600,000 square miles, or about the size of Alaska. A claim this size would be worth $12 billion given the modest estimate of $20 per acre, while at $100 per acre the value jumps to $40 billion.

Competition between private entities could be encouraged by allowing the first to develop a space transport system and Lunar base the largest claim, with smaller claims for subsequent groups. The second group, if and when one were able to also develop a transport system and manned base, might be allowed to claim 15% less land than the first group, the third group could claim 15% less than that, and so forth.

CONDITIONS FOR CLAIM RECOGNITION

Besides developing a reliable, government-approved space transportation system and sustainable Moon base, additional conditions could also be stipulated for rec-ognition of a claim. Representatives of the entity should be required to behave according to international norms, and the base itself should be a open to all and prohibit anti-competitive behavior. Regulations might even be put in place for protection of historical sites or other areas of special importance.

Another possibility might be allowing only a limited percentage of land sales revenue to go towards repaying the cost of establishing the base, with the balance being reserved to support the base itself until ways can be found to earn enough for self-sufficiency.

III. CAPABILITY OF PRIVATE INDUSTRY

The NASA Centennial Challenges program described in the NASA 2005 Appropriations Summary rewards private entities with annual prizes (up to a few tens of millions of dollars) for achieving "revolutionary, breakthrough accomplishments that advance solar system exploration and other NASA priorities...." NASA clearly believes that private industry can solve the complex problems associ-ated with Lunar missions and objectives.

Like space land claims recognition, the NASA Centennial Challenges program requires up-front private innovation, investment, and actual implementation as a prerequisite for receiving the award.

> By making awards based on actual achieve-ment, instead of proposals, NASA will tap inno-vators in academia, industry, and the public that do not normally work on NASA issues.

Consider the intense interest from private industry if a *multi-billion* dollar reward were at stake. A space land claims recognition protocol would offer the biggest Centennial Challenge of all, for the biggest achievement of all - without costing the taxpayers a cent.

IV. CONCLUSION

The costs of returning to the Moon and eventually going on to Mars will be enormous. Some future Congress or Administration may decide to divert the funding to other programs or purposes. Land claims recognition legislation should be enacted by Congress now to help free Lunar return missions from the uncertainty of government financing. Taxpayer relief would be an additional benefit, by shifting much of the financial burden for these missions from NASA to private industry.

The timeline for the government's Moon-to-Mars initiative spans decades and many Administrations. Making private industry the primary financier by integrating competition, the profit motive, and free enterprise would create long-term stability and a sense of assurance that the initiative will ultimately succeed.

1. According to this article, who can own land on the moon and how much is it worth?

2. What do you think about the author's belief in the power of private industry to catalyze space colonization?

"ALDRIN: MARS PIONEERS SHOULD NOT RETURN TO EARTH," BY IAN O'NEILL, FROM *UNIVERSE TODAY*, OCTOBER 23, 2008

Commenting on the strategy for the exploration of Mars, Buzz Aldrin, second man on the Moon and tireless space exploration advocate, has said that he believes the first explorers of the Red Planet should stay there. Following similar lines of the first European pioneers who settled in America, a small group of interplanetary explorers should expect to land, build, live and retire (probably even die) on Mars.

Setting up home on the Martian surface will be no easy thing (after all, the atmosphere is 100 times thinner than the Earth's and the planet has no magnetic field to protect colonists from the ravages of solar radiation), but Mars offers far greater potential as a habitable world than any other Solar System option.

40 years after Aldrin landed on the Moon, one can understand his frustration that there is no current manned space exploration program leaving Earth orbit. Perhaps a pioneering effort to Mars will make all the difference – if we succeed there, who knows where it might lead…

The subject of sending a manned expedition to Mars has always been a controversial one. Who do we send? How long should the mission last? Is sending one explorer an option (it would certainly be cheaper)? Do we make plans for a return mission? What about the health risks? Do we set up a human colony in the first instance? Is it REALLY worth the effort and money? But whether you like it or not, mankind will always have the urge to venture beyond Planet Earth and colonize other worlds (whether the funding or political will is there or not, but that's another story).

But how can it be done? There has been much speculation about the future of Mars exploration, and we are beginning to take the first baby-steps toward the ultimate goal – a manned mission. The Phoenix Mars lander is classed as a "scout mission" intended to aid the planning of future colonies; satellites such as the Mars Reconnaissance Orbiter (the clue is in the name – you have to do a bit of reconnaissance before sending in the troops!) has the The Compact Reconnaissance Imaging Spectrometer for Mars (CRISM) on board with the primary task of finding mineral deposits on the surface that might be of use to a manned settlement. Every mission we send to the Red Planet has some function to aid the planning of a future human presence on the Martian surface.

As if commenting on his personal experience of the Apollo Program, Buzz Aldrin has shared his views on manned exploration of Mars. As any manned spaceship could take up to 18 months to travel to Mars, Aldrin believes it makes more sense for the first mission to be a one-way trip. *"That's why you [should] send people there permanently," said Aldrin. "If we are not willing to do that, then I don't think we should just go once and have the expense of doing that and then stop."*

"If we are going to put a few people down there and ensure their appropriate safety, would you then go through all that trouble and then bring them back immediately, after a year, a year and a half?" Buzz added.

Currently, NASA and the European Space Agency has tentatively said they are planning for a trip to Mars by

2030 or 2040. The current idea is to send a small group of explorers (possibly six individuals) to Mars, but have all the life support systems and supplies already set up on the surface before they arrive. Once an outpost is established, more colonists can be sent out to join them. The first operational manned colony will probably be 30-strong.

However, these colonists will need to be unique individuals. *"They need to go there more with the psychology of knowing that you are a pioneering settler and you don't look forward to go back home again after a couple a years,"* Aldrin said. But that's not to say they'll never return to Earth. Years down the line, there may be the opportunity for a return mission, depending on technological advancements. *"At age 30, they are given an opportunity. If they accept, then we train them, at age 35, we send them. At age 65, who knows what advances have taken place. They can retire there, or maybe we can bring them back."*

Many will argue that a manned mission to Mars is a "waste of money," after all, why go through the expense and risk of sending humans when robots can do the same job. Aldrin disagrees with this stance, pointing out that it makes more sense to have humans on the ground, making on-the-spot decisions. I would argue that robotic explorers can only achieve so much; we can send the most advanced analysis equipment on board the most advanced robot, but there is no substitute for human ingenuity and experience. Far more science can be done on the Martian surface by an astronaut rather than a remote controlled robot. If life really does exist on the Martian surface, a man on Mars will find it far quicker than any rover.

Why else send man to Mars? To *do things that are innovative, new, pioneering,"* rather than letting manned space flight continue to be a disappointment, Buzz added. After all, the International Space Station hasn't lived up to many expectations, and the last time we walked on the Moon was in 1972… perhaps we need to start making some bold moves in the direction of Mars before we can consider ourselves to be a *space faring race.*

1. Why does Buzz Aldrin state that, in his opinion, the first space colonists to Mars should stay there permanently?

CHAPTER 4

WHAT THE MEDIA SAY

The general public's interest in the space program has waned since 1969, when hundreds of millions of people watched the first Moon landing on television. This should be of little surprise, as there has not been an event of comparable significance since then to serve as universal inspiration. Nonetheless, the media frequently report on technological progress and new discoveries, and the prospect of a person going to another celestial body again has rekindled some of this excitement. The news about spaceflight is no longer restricted to the efforts of the big national space agencies; private organizations and companies are making considerable progress as well and are likely to play a key role in humanity's future attempts to reach the stars. And, of course, the media will be there to document any new developments. If space flight actually brings astronauts to Mars or another planet, such a media event would dwarf the Moon landing—and cause a media sensation.

The articles in this chapter filter out specialized scientific knowledge to reach a wider audience, and speak to what a future with space colonization would look like.

"THE DEFINITIVE GUIDE TO TERRAFORMING," BY MATT WILLIAMS, FROM *UNIVERSE TODAY*, FEBRUARY 23, 2016

Terraforming. Chances are you've heard that word thrown around before, most likely in the context of some science fiction story. However, in recent years, thanks to renewed interest in space exploration, this word is being used in an increasingly serious manner. And rather than being talked about like a far-off prospect, the issue of terraforming other worlds is being addressed as a near-future possibility.

Whether it's Elon Musk claiming that humanity needs a "backup location" in order to survive, private ventures like MarsOne looking to send humans on a one-way mission to colonize the Red Planet, or space agencies like NASA and the ESA discussing the prospect of long-term habitability on Mars or the Moon, terraforming is yet another science fiction concept that appears to be moving towards science fact.

But just what does terraforming entail? Where exactly could we go about using this process? What kind of technology would we need? Does such technology already exist, or do we have to wait? How much in the way of resources would it take? And above all, what are the odds of it actually succeeding? Answering any or all of these questions requires that we do a bit of digging. Not only is terraforming a time-honored concept, but as it turns out, humanity already has quite a bit of experience in this area!

ORIGIN OF THE TERM:

To break it down, terraforming is the process whereby a hostile environment (i.e. a planet that is too cold, too hot, and/ or has an unbreathable atmosphere) is altered in order to be suitable for human life. This could involve modifying the temperature, atmosphere, surface topography, ecology – or all of the above – in order to make a planet or moon more "Earth-like".

The term was coined by Jack Williamson, an American science fiction writer who has also been called "the Dean of science fiction" (after the death of Robert Heinlein in 1988). The term appeared as part of a science-fiction story titled "Collision Orbit", which was published in the 1942 editions of the magazine *Astounding Science Fiction*. This is the first known mention of the concept, though there are examples of it appearing in fiction beforehand.

TERRAFORMING IN FICTION:

Science fiction is filled with examples of altering planetary environments to be more suitable to human life, many of which predate the scientific studies by many decades. For example, in H.G. Wells' *War of the Worlds*, he mentions at one point how the Martian invaders begin transforming Earth's ecology for the sake of long-term habitation.

In Olaf Stapleton's *Last And First Men* (1930), two chapters are dedicated to describing how humanity's descendants terraform Venus after Earth becomes uninhabitable; and in the process, commit genocide against the native aquatic life. By the 1950s and 60s, owing to the beginning of the Space Age, terraforming began to appear in works of science fiction with increasing frequency.

One such example is *Farmer in the Sky* (1950) by Robert A. Heinlein. In this novel, Heinlein offers a vision of Jupiter's moon Ganymede, which is being transformed into an agricultural settlement. This was a very significant work, in that it was the first where the concept of terraforming is presented as a serious and scientific matter, rather than the subject of mere fantasy.

In 1951, Arthur C. Clarke wrote the first novel in which the terraforming of Mars was presented in fiction. Titled *The Sands of Mars*, the story involves Martian settlers heating up the planet by converting Mars' moon Phobos into a second sun, and growing plants that break down the Martians sands in order to release oxygen. In his seminal book *2001: A Space Odyssey* – and it's sequel, *2010: Odyssey Two* – Clarke presents a race of ancient beings ("Firstborn") turning Jupiter into a second sun so that Europa will become a life-bearing planet.

Poul Anderson also wrote extensively about terraforming in the 1950s. In his 1954 novel, *The Big Rain*, Venus is altered through planetary engineering techniques over a very long period of time. The book was so influential that the term term "Big Rain" has since come to be synonimous with the terraforming of Venus. This was followed in 1958 by the *Snows of Ganymede*, where the Jovian moon's ecology is made habitable through a similar process.

In Issac Asimov's *Robot* series, colonization and terraforming is performed by a powerful race of humans known as "Spacers", who conduct this process on fifty planets in the known universe. In his *Foundation* series, humanity has effectively colonized every habitable planet in the galaxy and terraformed them to become part of the Galactic Empire.

In 1984, James Lovelock and Michael Allaby wrote what is considered by many to be one of the most influential books on terraforming. Titled *The Greening of Mars*, the novel explores the formation and evolution of planets, the origin of life, and Earth's biosphere. The terraforming models presented in the book actually foreshadowed future debates regarding the goals of terraforming.

In the 1990s, Kim Stanley Robinson released his famous trilogy that deals with the terraforming of Mars. Known as the *Mars Trilogy – Red Mars, Green Mars, Blue Mars –* this series centers on the transformation of Mars over the course of many generations into a thriving human civilization. This was followed up in 2012 with the release of *2312*, which deals with the colonization of the Solar System – including the terraforming of Venus and other planets.

Countless other examples can be found in popular culture, ranging from television and print to films and video games.

STUDY OF TERRAFORMING:

In an article published by the journal *Science* in 1961, famed astronomer Carl Sagan proposed using planetary engineering techniques to transform Venus. This involved seeding the atmosphere of Venus with algae, which would convert the atmosphere's ample supplies of water, nitrogen and carbon dioxide into organic compounds and reduce Venus' runaway greenhouse effect.

In 1973, he published an article in the journal Icarus titled "Planetary Engineering on Mars", where he proposed two scenarios for transforming Mars. These included transporting low albedo material and/or planting dark plants on the polar ice caps to ensure it absorbed more heat, melted, and converted the planet to more "Earth-like conditions".

In 1976, NASA addressed the issue of planetary engineering officially in a study titled "On the Habitability of Mars: An Approach to Planetary Ecosynthesis". The study concluded that photosynthetic organisms, the melting of the polar ice caps, and the introduction of greenhouse gases could all be used to create a warmer, oxygen and ozone-rich atmosphere.

The first conference session on terraforming, then referred to as "Planetary Modeling", was organized that same year.

And then in March of 1979, NASA engineer and author James Oberg organized the First Terraforming Colloquium – a special session at the Tenth Lunar and Planetary Science Conference, which is held annually in Houston, Texas. In 1981, Oberg popularized the concepts that were discussed at the colloquium in his book *New Earths: Restructuring Earth and Other Planets.*

In 1982, Planetologist Christopher McKay wrote "Terraforming Mars", a paper for the *Journal of the British Interplanetary Society.*In it, McKay discussed the prospects of a self-regulating Martian biosphere, which included both the required methods for doing so and ethics of it. This was the first time that the word terraforming was used in the title of a published article, and would henceforth become the preferred term.

This was followed by James Lovelock and Michael Allaby's *The Greening of Mars* in 1984. This book was one of the first to describe a novel method of warming Mars, where chlorofluorocarbons (CFCs) are added to the atmosphere in order to trigger global warming. This book motivated biophysicist Robert Haynes to begin promoting terraforming as part of a larger concept known as *Ecopoiesis*.

Derived from the Greek words *oikos* ("house") and *poiesis* ("production"), this word refers to the origin of an ecosystem. In the context of space exploration, it involves a form of planetary engineering where a sustainable ecosystem is fabricated from an otherwise sterile planet. As described by Haynes, this begins with the seeding of a planet with microbial life, which leads to conditions approaching that of a primordial Earth. This is then followed by the importation of plant life, which accelerates the production of oxygen, and culminates in the introduction of animal life.

In 2009, Kenneth Roy – an engineer with the US Department of Energy – presented his concept for a "Shell World" in a paper published with the Journal of British Interplanetary Sciences. Titled "Shell Worlds – An Approach

To Terraforming Moons, Small Planets and Plutoids", his paper explored the possibility of using a large "shell" to encase an alien world, keeping its atmosphere contained long enough for long-term changes to take root.

These and other concepts where a world is enclosed (in whole or in part) in an artificial shell in order to transform its environment is also known as "paraterraforming".

POTENTIAL SITES:

Within the Solar System, several possible locations exist that could be well-suited to terraforming. Consider the fact that besides Earth, Venus and Mars also lie within the Sun's Habitable Zone (aka. "Goldilocks Zone"). However, owing to Venus' runaway greenhouse effect, and Mars' lack of a magnetosphere, their atmospheres are either too thick and hot, or too thin and cold, to sustain life as we know it. However, this could theoretically be altered through the right kind of ecological engineering.

Other potential sites in the Solar System include some of the moons that orbit the gas giants. Several Jovian (i.e. in orbit of Jupiter) and Cronian (in orbit of Saturn) moons have an abundance of water ice, and scientists have speculated that if the surface temperatures were increased, viable atmospheres could be created through electrolysis and the introduction of buffer gases.

There is even speculation that Mercury and the Moon (or at least parts thereof) could be terraformed in order to be suitable for human settlement. In these cases, terraforming would require not only altering the surface, but perhaps also adjusting their rotation. In the end, each case presents its own share of advantages, challenges, and likelihoods for success. Let's consider them in order of distance from the Sun.

INNER SOLAR SYSTEM:

The terrestrial planets of our Solar System present the best possibilities for terraforming. Not only are they located closer to our Sun, and thus in a better position to absorb its energy, but they are also rich in silicates and minerals — which any future colonies will need to grow food and build settlements. And as already mentioned, two of these planets (Venus and Mars) are located within Earth's habitable zone.

MERCURY:

The vast majority of Mercury's surface is hostile to life, where temperatures gravitate between extremely hot and cold – i.e. 700 K (427 °C; 800 °F) 100 K (-173 °C; -280 °F). This is due to its proximity to the Sun, the almost total lack of an atmosphere, and its very slow rotation. However, at the poles, temperatures are consistently low -93 °C (-135 °F) due to it being permanently shadowed.

The presence of water ice and organic molecules in the northern polar region has also been confirmed thanks to data obtained by the MESSENGER mission. Colonies could therefore be constructed in the regions, and limited terraforming (aka. paraterraforming) could take place. For example, if domes (or a single dome) of sufficient size could be built over the Kandinsky, Prokofiev, Tolkien and Tryggvadottir craters, the norther region could be altered for human habitation.

Theoretically, this could be done by using mirrors to redirect sunlight into the domes which would gradually raise the temperature. The water ice would then melt, and when combined with organic molecules and finely ground sand, soil could be made. Plants could then be grown to produce oxygen, which combined with nitrogen gas, would produce a breathable atmosphere.

VENUS:

As "Earth's Twin", there are many possibilities and advantages to terraforming Venus. The first to propose this was Sagan with his 1961 article in *Science*. However, subsequent discoveries – such as the high concentrations of sulfuric acid in Venus' clouds – made this idea unfeasible. Even if algae could survive in such an atmosphere, converting the extremely dense clouds of CO_2 into oxygen would result in an over-dense oxygen environment.

In addition, graphite would become a by-product of the chemical reactions, which would likely form into a thick powder on the surface. This would become CO_2 again through combustion, thus restarting the entire greenhouse effect. However, more recent proposals have been made that advocate using carbon sequestration techniques, which are arguably much more practical.

In these scenarios, chemical reactions would be relied on to convert Venus' atmosphere to something breathable while also reducing its density. In one scenario, hydrogen and iron aerosol would be introduced to convert the CO_2 in the atmosphere into graphite and water. This water would then fall to the surface, where it cover roughly 80% of the planet – due to Venus having little variation in elevation.

Another scenario calls for the introduction of vast amounts of calcium and magnesium into the atmosphere. This would sequester carbon in the form of calcium and magnesium carbonites. And advantage to this plan is that Venus already has deposits of both minerals in its mantle, which could then be exposed to the atmosphere through drilling. However, most of the minerals would have to come from off-world in order to reduce the temperature and pressure to sustainable levels.

Yet another proposal is to freeze the atmospheric carbon dioxide down to the point of liquefaction – where it forms dry ice – and letting it accumulate on the surface. Once there, it could be buried and would remain in a solid state due to pressure, and even mined for local and off-world use. And then there is the possibility of bombarding the surface with icy comets (which could be mined from one of Jupiter's or Saturn's moons) to create a liquid ocean on the surface, which would sequester carbon and aid in any other of the above processes.

Last, there is the scenario in which Venus' dense atmosphere could be removed. This could be characterized as the most direct approach to thinning an atmosphere which is far too dense for human occupation. By colliding large comets or asteroids into the surface, some of the dense CO_2 clouds could be blasted into space, thus leaving less atmosphere to be converted.

A slower method could be achieved using mass drivers (aka. electromagnetic catapults) or space elevators, which would gradually scoop up the atmosphere and either lift it into space, or fire it away from the surface.

And beyond altering or removing the atmosphere, there are also concepts that call for reducing the heat and pressure by either limiting sunlight (i.e. with solar shades) or altering the planet's rotational velocity.

The concept of solar shades involves using either a series of small spacecraft or a single large lens to divert sunlight from a planet's surface, thus reducing global temperatures. For Venus, which absorbs twice as much sunlight as Earth, solar radiation is believed to have played a major role in the runaway greenhouse effect that has made it what it is today.

Such a shade could be space-based, located in the Sun–Venus L1 Lagrangian Point, where it would not only prevent some sunlight from reaching Venus, but also serve to reduce the amount of radiation Venus is exposed to. Alternately, solar shades or reflectors could be placed in the atmosphere or on the surface. This could consist of large reflective balloons, sheets of carbon nanotubes or graphene, or low-albedo material.

Placing shades or reflectors in the atmosphere offers two advantages: for one, atmospheric reflectors could be built in-situ, using locally-sourced carbon. Second, Venus' atmosphere is dense enough that such structures could easily float atop the clouds. However, the amount of material would have to be large and would have to remain in place long after the atmosphere had been modified. Also, since Venus already has highly reflective clouds, any approach would have to significantly surpass its current albedo (0.65) to make a difference.

Also, the idea of speeding up Venus' rotation has been floating around as a possible means of terraforming. If Venus could be spun-up to the point where its diurnal (day-night) cycle were similar to Earth's, the planet might just begin to generate a stronger magnetic field. This would have the effect of reducing the amount of solar wind (and hence radiation) from reaching the surface, thus making it safer for terrestrial organisms.

THE MOON:

As Earth's closest celestial body, colonizing the Moon would be comparatively easy compared to other bodies. But when it comes to terraforming the Moon, the possibilities and challenges closely resemble those of Mercury. For starters, the Moon has an atmosphere that is so thin that it can only be referred to as an exosphere. What's more, the volatile elements that are necessary for life are in short supply (i.e. hydrogen, nitrogen, and carbon).

These problems could be addressed by capturing comets that contain water ices and volatiles and crashing them into the surface. The comets would sublimate, dispersing these gases and water vapor to create an the atmosphere. These impacts would also liberate water that is contained in the lunar regolith, which could eventually accumulate on the surface to form natural bodies of water.

The transfer of momentum from these comet would also get the Moon rotating more rapidly, speeding up its rotation so that it would no longer be tidally-locked. A Moon that was sped up to rotate once on its axis every 24 hours would have a steady diurnal cycle, which would make colonization and adapting to life on the Moon easier.

There is also the possibility of paraterraforming parts of the Moon in a way that would be similar to terra-

145

forming Mercury's polar region. In the Moon's case, this would take place in the Shackleton Crater, where scientists have already found evidence of water ice. Using solar mirrors and a dome, this crater could be turned into a micro-climate where plants could be grown and a breathable atmosphere created.

MARS:

When it comes to terraforming, Mars is the most popular destination. There are several reasons for this, ranging from its proximity to Earth, its similarities to Earth, and the fact that it once had an environment that was very similar to Earth's – which included a thicker atmosphere and the presence of warm, flowing water on the surface. Lastly, it is currently believed that Mars may have additional sources of water beneath its surface.

In brief, Mars has a diurnal and seasonal cycle that are very close what we experience here on Earth. In the former case, a single day on Mars lasts 24 hours and 40 minutes. In the latter case, and owing to Mars similarly tilted axis (25.19° compared to Earth's 23°), Mars experiences seasonal changes that are very similar to Earth's. Though a single season on Mars lasts roughly twice as long, the temperature variation that results is very similar – ±178 °C (320°F) compared to Earth's ±160 °C (278°F).

Beyond these, Mars would need to undergo vast transformations in order for human beings to live on its surface. The atmosphere would need to be thickened drastically, and its composition would need to be changed. Currently, Mars' atmosphere is composed of

96% carbon dioxide, 1.93% argon and 1.89% nitrogen, and the air pressure is equivalent to only 1% of Earth's at sea level.

Above all, Mars lacks a magnetosphere, which means that its surface receives significantly more radiation than we are used to here on Earth. In addition, it is believed that Mars once had a magnetosphere, and that the disappearance of this magnetic field led to solar wind to stripping away Mars' atmosphere. This in turn is what led Mars to become the cold, desiccated place it is today.

Ultimately, this means that in order for the planet to become habitable by human standards, it's atmosphere would need to be significantly thickened and the planet significantly warmed. The composition of the atmosphere would need to change as well, from the current CO_2-heavy mix to an nitrogen-oxygen balance of about 70/30. And above all, the atmosphere would need to be replenished every so often to compensate for loss.

Luckily, the first three requirements are largely complimentary, and present a wide range of possible solutions. For starters, Mars' atmosphere could be thickened and the planet warmed by bombarding its polar regions with meteors. These would cause the poles to melt, releasing their deposits of frozen carbon dioxide and water into the atmosphere and triggering a greenhouse effect.

The introduction of volatile elements, such as ammonia and methane, would also help to thicken the atmosphere and trigger warming. Both could be mined from the icy moons of the outer Solar System, particularly from the moons of Ganymede, Callisto, and Titan. These could also be delivered to the surface via meteoric impacts.

After impacting on the surface, the ammonia ice would sublimate and break down into hydrogen and nitrogen – the hydrogen interacting with he CO_2 to form water and graphite, while the nitrogen acts as a buffer gas. The methane, meanwhile, would act as a greenhouse gas that would further enhance global warming. In addition, the impacts would throw tons of dust into the air, further fueling the warming trend.

In time, Mars' ample supplies of water ice – which can be found not only in the poles but in vast subsurface deposits of permafrost – would all sublimate to form warm, flowing water. And with significantly increased air pressure and a warmer atmosphere, humans might be able to venture out onto the surface without the need for pressure suits.

However, the atmosphere will still need to be converted into something breathable. This will be far more time-consuming, as the process of converting the atmospheric CO_2 into oxygen gas will likely take centuries. In any case, several possibilities have been suggested, which include converting the atmosphere through photosynthesis – either with cyanobacteria or Earth plants and lichens.

Other suggestions include building orbital mirrors, which would be placed near the poles and direct sunlight onto the surface to trigger a cycle of warming by causing the polar ice caps to melt and release their CO_2 gas. Using dark dust from Phobos and Deimos to reduce the surface's albedo, thus allowing it to absorb more sunlight, has also been suggested.

In short, there are plenty of options for terraforming Mars. And many of them, if not being readily available, are at least on the table…

OUTER SOLAR SYSTEM:

Beyond the Inner Solar System, there are several sites that would make for good terraforming targets as well. Particularly around Jupiter and Saturn, there are several sizable moons – some of which are larger than Mercury – that have an abundance of water in the form of ice (and in some cases, maybe even interior oceans).

At the same time, many of these same moons contain other necessary ingredients for functioning ecosystems, such as frozen volatiles – like ammonia and methane. Because of this, and as part of our ongoing desire to explore farther out into our Solar System, many proposals have been made to seed these moons with bases and research stations. Some plans even include possible terraforming to make them suitable for long-term habitation.

THE JOVIAN MOONS:

Jupiter's largest moons, Io, Europa, Ganymede and Callisto – known as the Galileans, after their founder (Galileo Galilei) – have long been the subject of scientific interest. For decades, scientists have speculated about the possible existence of a subsurface ocean on Europa, based on theories about the planet's tidal heating (a consequence of its eccentric orbit and orbital resonance with the other moons).

Analysis of images provided by the *Voyager 1* and *Galileo* probes added weight to this theory, showing regions where it appeared that the subsurface ocean had melted through. What's more, the presence of this warm water ocean has also led to speculation about the existence of life beneath Europa's icy crust – possibly around hydrothermal vents at the core-mantle boundary.

Because of this potential for habitability, Europa has also been suggested as a possible site for terraforming. As the argument goes, if the surface temperature could be increased, and the surface ice melted, the entire planet could become a ocean world. Sublimation of the ice, which would release water vapor and gaseous volatiles, would then be subject to electrolysis (which already produces a thin oxygen atmosphere).

However, Europa has no magnetosphere of its own, and lies within Jupiter's powerful magnetic field. As a result, its surface is exposed to significant amounts of radiation – 540 rem of radiation per day compared to about 0.0030 rem per year here on Earth – and any atmosphere we create would begin to be stripped away by Jupiter. Ergo, radiation shielding would need to be put in place that could deflect the majority of this radiation.

And then there is Ganymede, the third most-distant of Jupiter's Galilean moons. Much like Europa, it is a potential site of terraforming, and presents numerous advantages. For one, it is the largest moon in our Solar System, larger than our own moon and even larger that the planet Mercury. In addition, it also has ample supplies of water ice, is believed to have an interior ocean, and even has its own magnetosphere.

Hence, if the surface temperature were increased and the ice sublimated, Ganymede's atmosphere could be thickened. Like Europa, it would also become an ocean planet, and its own magnetosphere would allow for it to hold on to more of its atmosphere. However, Jupiter's magnetic field still exerts a powerful influence over the planet, which means radiation shields would still be needed.

Lastly, there is Callisto, the fourth-most distant of the Galileans. Here too, abundant supplies of water ice, volatiles, and the possibility of an interior ocean all point towards the potential for habitability. But in Callisto's case, there is the added bonus of it being beyond Jupiter's magnetic field, which reduces the threat of radiation and atmospheric loss.

The process would begin with surface heating, which would sublimate the water ice and Callisto's supplies of frozen ammonia. From these oceans, electrolysis would lead to the formation of an oxygen-rich atmosphere, and the ammonia could be converted into nitrogen to act as a buffer gas. However, since the majority of Callisto is ice, it would mean that the planet would lose considerable mass and have no continents. Again, an ocean planet would result, necessitated floating cities or massive colony ships.

THE CRONIANS MOONS:

Much like the Jovian Moons, Saturn's Moons (also known as the Cronian) present opportunities for terraforming. Again, this is due to the presence of water ice, interior oceans, and volatile elements. Titan, Saturn's largest moon, also has an abundance of methane that comes in liquid form (the methane lakes around its northern polar region) and in gaseous form in its atmosphere. Large caches of ammonia are also believed to exist beneath he surface ice.

Titan is also the only natural satellite to have a dense atmosphere (one and half times the pressure of Earth's) and the only planet outside of Earth where the atmosphere is nitrogen-rich. Such a thick atmosphere would mean that it would be far easier to equalize pressure for habitats on the planet. What's more, scientists believe this atmosphere is a prebiotic environment rich in organic chemistry – i.e. similar to Earth's early atmosphere (only much colder).

As such, converting it to something Earth-like would be feasible. First, the surface temperature would need to be increased. Since Titan is very distant from the Sun, and already has an abundance of greenhouse gases, this could only be accomplished through orbital mirrors. This would sublimate the surface ice, releasing ammonia beneath, which would lead to more heating.

The next step would involve converting the atmosphere to something breathable. As already noted, Titan's atmosphere is nitrogen-rich, which would remove the need for introducing a buffer gas. And with the availability of water, oxygen could be introduced by generating it through electrolysis. At the same time, the methane and other hydrocarbons would have to be sequestered, in order to prevent an explosive mixture with the oxygen.

But given the thickness and multi-layered nature of Titan's ice, which is estimated to account for half of its mass, the moon would be very much an ocean planet- i.e. with no continents or landmasses to build on. So once again, any habitats would have to take the form of either floating platforms or large ships.

Enceladus is another possibility, thanks to the recent discovery of a subsurface ocean. Analysis by the

Cassini space probe of the water plumes erupting from its southern polar region also indicated the presence of organic molecules. As such, terraforming it would be similar to terraforming Jupiter's moon of Europa, and would yield a similar ocean moon.

Again, this would likely have to involve orbital mirrors, given Enceladus' distance from our Sun. Once the ice began to sublimate, electrolysis would generate oxygen gas. The presence of ammonia in the subsurface ocean would also be released, helping to raise the temperature and serving as a source of nitrogen gas, with which to buffer the atmosphere.

EXOPLANETS:

In addition to the Solar System, extra-solar planets (aka. exoplanets) are also potential sites for terraforming. Of the 1,941 confirmed exoplanets discovered so far, these planets are those that have been designated "Earth-like. In other words, they are terrestrial planets that have atmospheres and, like Earth, occupy the region around a star where the average surface temperature allows for liquid water (aka. habitable zone).

The first planet confirmed by Kepler to have an average orbital distance that placed it within its star's habitable zone was Kepler-22b. This planet is located about 600 light years from Earth in the constellation of Cygnus, was first observed on May 12th, 2009 and then confirmed on Dec 5th, 2011. Based on all the data obtained, scientists believe that this world is roughly 2.4 times the radius of Earth, and is likely covered in oceans or has a liquid or gaseous outer shell.

In addition, there are star systems with multiple "Earth-like" planets occupying their habitable zones. Gliese 581 is a good example, a red dwarf star that is located 20.22 light years away from Earth in the Libra constellation. Here, three confirmed and two possible planets exist, two of which are believed to orbit within the star's habitable zone. These include the confirmed planet Gliese 581 d and the hypothetical Gliese 581 g.

Tau Ceti is another example. This G-class star, which is located roughly 12 light years from Earth in the constellation Cetus, has five possible planets orbiting it. Two of these are Super-Earths that are believed to orbit the star's habitable zone – Tau Ceti e and Tau Ceti f. However, Tau Ceti e is believed to be too close for anything other than Venus-like conditions to exist on its surface.

In all cases, terraforming the atmospheres of these planet's would most likely involve the same techniques used to terraform Venus and Mars, though to varying degrees. For those located on the outer edge of their habitable zones, terraforming could be accomplished by introducing greenhouse gases or covering the surface with low albedo material to trigger global warming. On the other end, solar shades and carbon sequestering techniques could reduce temperatures to the point where the planet is considered hospitable.

POTENTIAL BENEFITS:

When addressing the issue of terraforming, there is the inevitable question – "why should we?" Given the expenditure in resources, the time involved, and other challenges that naturally arise (see below), what reasons are there to engage in terraforming? As already mentioned, there is the reasons cited by Musk, about the need to have a "backup location" to prevent any particular cataclysm from claiming all of humanity.

Putting aside for the moment the prospect of nuclear holocaust, there is also the likelihood that life will become untenable on certain parts of our planet in the coming century. As the NOAA reported in March of 2015, carbon dioxide levels in the atmosphere have now surpassed 400 ppm, a level not seen since the the Plio-cene Era – when global temperatures and sea level were significantly higher.

And as a series of scenarios computed by NASA show, this trend is likely to continue until 2100, and with serious consequences. In one scenario, carbon dioxide emissions will level off at about 550 ppm toward the end of the century, resulting in an average temperature increase of 2.5 °C (4.5 °F). In the second scenario, carbon dioxide emissions rise to about 800 ppm, resulting in an average increase of about 4.5 °C (8 °F). Whereas the increases predicted in the first scenario are sustainable, in the latter scenario, life will become untenable on many parts of the planet.

As a result of this, creating a long-term home for humanity on Mars, the Moon, Venus, or elsewhere in the Solar System may be necessary. In addition to offering us other locations from which to extract resources, cultivate food, and as a possible outlet for population pressures, having colonies on other worlds could mean the differ-ence between long-term survival and extinction.

There is also the argument that humanity is already well-versed in altering planetary environments. For centuries, humanity's reliance on industrial machinery, coal and fossil fuels has had a measurable effect Earth's environment. And whereas the Greenhouse Effect that we have triggered here was not deliberate, our experience and knowledge in creating it here on Earth could be put to good use on planets where surface temperatures need to be raised artificially.

In addition, it has also been argued that working with environments where there is a runaway Greenhouse Effect – i.e. Venus – could yield valuable knowledge that could in turn be used here on Earth. Whether it is the use of extreme bacteria, introducing new gases, or mineral elements to sequester carbon, testing these methods out on Venus could help us to combat Climate Change here at home.

It has also been argued that Mars' similarities to Earth are a good reason to terraform it. Essentially, Mars once resembled Earth, until its atmosphere was stripped away, causing it to lose virtually all the liquid water on its surface. Ergo, terraforming it would be tantamount to returning it to its once-warm and watery glory. The same argument could be made of Venus, where efforts to alter it would restore it to what it was before a runaway Greenhouse Effect turned it into the harsh, extremely hot world it is today.

Last, but not least, there is argument that colonizing the Solar System could usher in an age of "post-scarcity". If humanity were to build outposts and based on other worlds, mine the asteroid belt and harvest the resources of the Outer Solar System, we would effectively have enough minerals, gases, energy, and water resources to last us indefinitely. It could also help trigger a massive acceleration in human development, defined by leaps and bounds in technological and social progress.

POTENTIAL CHALLENGES:

When it comes right down to it, all of the scenarios listed above suffer from one or more of the following problems:

- They are not possible with existing technology
- They require a massive commitment of resources
- They solve one problem, only to create another
- They do not offer a significant return on the investment
- They would take a really, REALLY long time

Case in point, all of the potential ideas for terraforming Venus and Mars involve infrastructure that does not yet exist and would be very expensive to create. For instance, the orbital shade concept that would cool Venus calls for a structure that would need to be four times the diameter of Venus itself (if it were positioned at L1). It would therefore require megatons of material, all of which would have to be assembled on site.

In contrast, increasing the speed of Venus's rotation would require energy many orders of magnitude greater than the construction of orbiting solar mirrors. As with removing Venus' atmosphere, the process would also require a significant number of impactors that would have to be harnessed from the outer solar System – mainly from the Kuiper Belt.

In order to do this, a large fleet of spaceships would be needed to haul them, and they would need to be equipped with advanced drive systems that could make the trip in a reasonable amount of time. Currently, no such drive systems exist, and conventional methods – ranging from ion engines to chemical propellants – are neither fast or economical enough.

To illustrate, NASA's *New Horizons* mission took more than 11 years to get make its historic rendezvous with Pluto in the Kuiper Belt, using conventional rockets and the gravity-assist method. Meanwhile, the *Dawn* mission, which relied relied on ionic propulsion, took almost four years to reach Vesta in the Asteroid Belt. Neither method is practical for making repeated trips to the Kuiper Belt and hauling back icy comets and asteroids, and humanity has nowhere near the number of ships we would need to do this.

The Moon's proximity makes it an attractive option for terraforming. But again, the resources needed – which would likely include several hundred comets – would again need to be imported from the outer Solar System. And while Mercury's resources could be harvested in-situ or brought from Earth to paraterraform its northern polar region, the concept still calls for a large fleet of ships and robot builders which do not yet exist.

The outer Solar System presents a similar problem. In order to begin terraforming these moons, we would need infrastructure between here and there, which would mean bases on the Moon, Mars, and within the Asteroid Belt. Here, ships could refuel as they transport materials to the Jovian sand Cronian systems, and resources could be harvested from all three of these locations as well as within the systems themselves.

But of course, it would take many, many generations (or even centuries) to build all of that, and at considerable cost. Ergo, any attempts at terraforming the outer Solar

System would have to wait until humanity had effectively colonized the inner Solar System. And terraforming the Inner Solar System will not be possible until humanity has plenty of space hauler on hand, not to mention fast ones!

The necessity for radiation shields also presents a problem. The size and cost of manufacturing shields that could deflect Jupiter's magnetic field would be astronomical. And while the resources could be harvest from the nearby Asteroid Belt, transporting and assembling them in space around the Jovian Moons would again require many ships and robotic workers. And again, there would have to be extensive infrastructure between Earth and the Jovian system before any of this could proceed.

As for item three, there are plenty of problems that could result from terraforming. For instance, transforming Jupiter's and Saturn's moons into ocean worlds could be pointless, as the volume of liquid water would constitute a major portion of the moon's overall radius. Combined with their low surface gravities, high orbital velocities and the tidal effects of their parent planets, this could lead to severely high waves on their surfaces. In fact, these moons could become totally unstable as a result of being altered.

There is also several questions about the ethics of terraforming. Basically, altering other planets in order to make them more suitable to human needs raises the natural question of what would happen to any lifeforms already living there. If in fact Mars and other Solar System bodies have indigenous microbial (or more complex) life, which many scientists suspect, then altering their ecology could impact or even wipe out these lifeforms. In short, future colonists and terrestrial engineers would effectively be committing genocide.

Another argument that is often made against terra-forming is that any effort to alter the ecology of another planet does not present any immediate benefits. Given the cost involved, what possible incentive is there to commit so much time, resources and energy to such a project? While the idea of utilizing the resources of the Solar System makes sense in the long-run, the short-term gains are far less tangible.

Basically, harvested resources from other worlds is not economically viable when you can extract them here at home for much less. And real-estate is only the basis of an economic model if the real-estate itself is desirable. While MarsOne has certainly shown us that there are plenty of human beings who are willing to make a one-way trip to Mars, turning the Red Planet, Venus or elsewhere into a "new frontier" where people can buy up land will first require some serious advances in technology, some serious terraforming, or both.

As it stands, the environments of Mars, Venus, the Moon, and the outer Solar System are all hostile to life as we know it. Even with the requisite commitment of resources and people willing to be the "first wave", life would be very difficult for those living out there. And this situation would not change for centuries or even millennia. Like it not, transforming a planet's ecology is very slow, laborious work.

CONCLUSION

So... after considering all of the places where human-ity *could* colonize and terraform, what it *would* take to make that happen, and the difficulties in doing so, we are once again left with one important question. Why *should* we? Assuming that our very survival is not at stake, what possible incentives are there for humanity to become an interplanetary (or interstellar) species?

Perhaps there is no good reason. Much like sending astronauts to the Moon, taking to the skies, and climbing the highest mountain on Earth, colonizing other planets may be nothing more than something we feel we need to do. Why? Because we can! Such a reason has been good enough in the past, and it will likely be sufficient again in the not-too-distant future.

This should is no way deter us from considering the ethical implications, the sheer cost involved, or the cost-to-benefit ratio. But in time, we might find that we have no choice but to get out there, simply because Earth is just becoming too stuffy and crowded for us!

1. Which planets are the best candidates for space colonization? Which difficulties do they present?

"THE VALUE OF SPACE EXPLORATION," BY FRASER CAIN, FROM *UNIVERSE TODAY*, APRIL 11, 2008

Read any debate about space exploration, and this question will invariably come up. *"Why should we be spending money exploring space when there are so many problems here on Earth that we need to solve first?"* It's a tricky one.

I've got a simple answer; space exploration is awesome. Come on, think of space ships traveling to other worlds – that's really cool.

Okay, perhaps I've got too simplistic an argument, so I turned to the astrosphere and posed the question to other space bloggers. Here's what they had to say...

ALUN SALT – ARCHEOASTRONOMY

Historical materials suggest that there wasn't such sharp division between earth and sky in the ancient world. Instead there was one cosmos. Space exploration reveals that while there isn't a divine link between the heavens and the earth, it is true that what happens up there can affect what happens down here. It would be useful to know about the cosmos, rather than just be a victim of it.

MARK WHITTINGTON – CURMUDGEONS CORNER

What is the value of space exploration? Inherent in exploration of all types is the opportunities that it opens up to the people doing the exploring. For some it is the opportunity to gain new knowledge. For others it is the opportunity to create wealth and expand commerce. For still others the opportunity lies is trancendence, to grow spirtually and to gain a greater appreciation of the universe.

ALAN BOYLE – MSNBC COSMIC LOG

I've been getting a healthy dose of the American revolution lately, between watching HBO's "John Adams" miniseries and reading David McCullough's "1776," and that may be the reason I'm thinking of this in terms of pledging "our lives, our fortunes and our sacred honor" rather than just thinking in terms of paying taxes. I like to think of the reasons for making that pledge, in terms of the push to outer space, as the five E's (plus examples): exploration (to the moon and Mars), entertainment (cool Hubble pictures), energy (space solar power and asteroid mines), empire building (defending the high frontier) and extinction avoidance (fending off space rocks, and getting off this rock).

STEINN SIGURDSSON – DYNAMICS OF CATS

Because: we look out, and wonder, and explore;
and we do what little we can on the margin of our busy lives to explore the bigger universe, today;
and that is one of the things that makes life worth living, and gives us hope that the future can be better, for us and for future generations.

ETHAN SIEGEL – STARTS WITH A BANG

This is like asking why we should spend money on making our city better when there are so many problems here in our own homes. Or why we should spend money on understanding our whole world when there are so many problems here in our own country. Space is something that we are not only a part of, but that encompasses and affects all of us. Learning about the grandest scales of our lives — about the things that are larger than us and will go on relatively unaffected by whatever we do — that has value! And it might not have a value that I can put a price tag on, but in terms of unifying everyone, from people in my city to people in a foreign country to people or intelligences on other planets or in other galaxies, space exploration is something that is the great equalizer. And the knowledge, beauty, and understanding that we get from it is something that one person, group, or nation doesn't get to keep to itself; what we learn about the Universe can be, should be, and if we do our jobs right, will be equally available to everyone, everywhere. This is where our entire world came from, and this is the abyss our entire world will eventually return to. And learning about that, exploring that, and gaining even a small understanding of that, has the ability to give us a perspective that we can never gain just by looking insularly around our little blue rock.

BILL DUNFORD – RIDING WITH ROBOTS ON THE HIGH FRONTIER

Why should we worry about what's going on outside the cave? We have so many problems here inside in the cave.

Why should we waste time trying to figure out agriculture? We have so much work to do hunting and gathering.

Why should we spend so much effort messing about in boats? We have so many issues here on the land.

Why should we fiddle with those computers? There is so much calculating that still needs to be done with these pencils.

Why should we explore space? We have so many problems here on Earth.

The answer to all these questions is the same: reaching for new heights often creates new solutions, new opportunity and elevated hope back on the ground.

We should NOT spend indiscriminately in space. But moderately-funded space exploration — as one small part of an overall program of basic scientific research — has blessed lives in many ways over the years, from satellites measuring drought conditions to new imaging techniques in hospitals to global communication.

BRIAN WANG – NEXT BIG FUTURE

Lack of a space program will not solve anything else faster and a well planned program [not what we have been doing] can deliver massive benefits. History shows the logical flaw.

There has been no historical example of any group "solving all of their problems before embarking on exploration/expansion/major project". The solve all problems locally before advancing has not been shown to be a successful strategy. There has been major examples where the imperfect/highly flawed expander had major advantages over the non-expander (who was also flawed). The biggest one is China had the largest ocean going fleet in 1400s. Then the emperor destroyed that fleet. The Western nations came a few hundred years later and forced China to give up Hong Kong and Macau for 99 years. The Europeans colonized North America and expanded economies because of those policies. The world has about a 60 trillion/year economy. There is not a shortage of resources in money or people to target problems. Well funded, well planned and well executed efforts can be directed at all of the problems simultaneously. Just putting ten times, a hundred times or a million times more money does not convert a failing plan, project against hunger, poverty, corruption into a successful plan. We better plans and better thinking.

Space exploration and development has had a lot of waste and a lack of purpose and a good plan. A strong case can be made that the overall purpose of the space programs have been one aspect of political pork with minimal space efforts and the name space program. Clearly the space shuttle and the space station have vastly under delivered for the money spent on them.

Strategies for successful space development: Focus on lowering the cost and the purpose of colonization and industrialization and commerce (tourism etc…)

If lowering the cost is best [done] with more robots then use robots first or mainly. [D]o not force the manned program until costs go down.

[F]uel depots in space (bring the costs down closer to the cost of LEO $2000/kg)

More nuclear propulsion and non-chemical systems (mirrored laser arrays for launches).

IAN O'NEILL – ASTROENGINE

Being an astrophysicist and space colonization advocate, my natural, basic and very quick answer is: to explore the undiscovered. It is a very basic human trait to want to explore, why limit our horizons to the surface of the Earth when there are infinite possibilities for development of the human race amongst the stars? We could be on the verge of realising that this step into the cosmos is a very natural progression for us. To borrow a quote from Stephen Hawking:

> "We once thought we were at the centre of the Universe. Then we thought the sun was. Eventually, we realised we were just on the edge of one of billions of galaxies. Soon we may have to humbly accept that our 3D universe is just one of many multi-dimensional worlds."

Looking back on the 21st century, when we have established a presence throughout the solar system, future generations will view our "proto-space" selves much like how we look upon the pioneers and explorers of the 16th century who colonized the strange but fruitful lands of the Americas. Back then, the Earth was flat. Like then, the going will be tough and the rewards of "leaving the nest" will not be fully realised until we make that bold push into a new era of discovery. Space exploration is as natural as colonizing the continents; it may look costly from the outset, but in the end we'll all benefit and evolve.

JOHN BENAC – ACTION FOR SPACE

Mankind's expansion to the Moon and Mars will serve as a shocking and unifying symbol that lifts the even the poorest soul's belief in what they, as a human, can accomplish. 7 billion people each raise their belief in what man, individually and in groups, can accomplish, and the collective change in positive self-confidence provides a new ability and impetus to solve all other problems on Earth.

PHIL PLAIT – BAD ASTRONOMY

First, the question of why spend money there when we have problems here is a false dichotomy. We have enough money to work on problems here and in space! We just don't seem to choose to, which is maddening. $12 million an hour is spent in Iraq; the US government chose to do that instead of fix many problems that could have been solved with that money. NASA is less than 1% of the US budget, so it's best to pick your fights wisely here.

Second, space exploration is necessary. We learn so much from it! Early attempts discovered the van Allen radiation belts (with America's first satellite!). Later satellites found the ozone hole, letting us know we were damaging our ecosystem. Weather prediction via satellites is another obvious example, as well as global communication, TV, GPS, and much more.

If you want to narrow it down to exploring other planets and the Universe around us, again we can give the practical answer that the more we learn about our space environment, the more we learn about the Earth itself. Examining the Sun led us to understand that its magnetic field connects with ours, sometimes with disastrous results… yet we can fortify ourselves against the danger, should we so choose. Space exploration may yet save us from an asteroid impact, too. Spreading our seed to other worlds may eventually save the human race.

But I'm with Fraser. These are all good reasons, and there are many, many more. But it is the very nature of humans to explore! We could do nothing in our daily lives but look no farther than the ends of our noses. We could labor away in a gray, listless, dull world.

Or we can look up, look out to the skies, see what wonders are there, marvel at exploding stars, majestic galaxies, ringed worlds, and perhaps planets like our own. That gives us beauty and joy in our world, and adds a depth and dimension that we might otherwise miss.

Space exploration is cheap. Not exploring is always very, very expensive.

ASTROPROF – ASTROPROF'S PAGE

Space exploration is important BECAUSE we have problems here on Earth. We need to expand and grow as a species. Our planet has limited resources, and we need the resources availible in the Solar System as a whole if we are to use them to solve our problems here. The technological advances developed for space exploration also go to solving other problems on Earth. And, on top of all that, Earth is a planet. Understanding planets helps us understand our own planet. And, Earth is affected and influenced by external forces. Understanding those things also helps us to understand our planet, and allows us to adapt to changes that occur naturally or that we create.

ROBERT PEARLMAN – COLLECTSPACE

Many of the problems we have on Earth are rooted in our need for new ideas. From medical advancements to political diplomacy, it often takes a new perspective to find the answer. Space exploration offers the rare opportunity to look inwards while pushing out. The photographs sent back of the Earth as a "fragile blue marble", a whole sphere for the first time, gave birth to the environmental movement. Astronauts, regardless of their home nation, have returned to Earth with a new world view, without borders. But the perspective isn't limited to those who leave the planet. When Neil Armstrong and Buzz Aldrin walked on the Moon, "mankind" took on a new appreciation for all of humanity. It was "we" who went, even if "we" were not living in the United States. That sense of unity was recognized by the Apollo 11 crew upon their return to the planet: Buzz turned to Neil and commented, "We missed the whole thing…"

ROBERT SIMPSON – ORBITING FROG

The value of knowing about things is not quantifiable. We can qualitatively say that as we have become more knowledge-able, we have become better prepared for the things that come our way. We are more able to grow and to make progress by knowing more about the world we live in. Our planet is just one of many in a solar system that is also just one of many.

The cost of human exploration, and the risks involved, are often discussed. However everyone would seem to agree that until a human being had set foot on the Moon, we had not really been there. Likewise, it will not be until humans stand on Mars, that we have really visited the planet. Science can be done by robots and probes, but experience can still only be obtained by human beings.

RYAN ANDERSON – THE MARTIAN CHRONICLES

The List:
1. Perspective
2. Protecting and Understanding our World

3. Inspiration

4. The Economy

5. Exploration

6. New Technology

7. Answering the Big Questions

8. International Collaboration

9. Long-Term Survival

Of course, that's just our opinion. What's yours?

1. How would you answer the question that these space bloggers were posed: "Why should we be spending money exploring space when there are so many problems here on Earth that we need to solve first?"

"A GOLDEN AGE OF EXOPLANET SCIENCE," BY JEFF FOUST, FROM *THE SPACE REVIEW*, JANUARY 14, 2013

The term "golden age" gets thrown around a lot to refer to an era of particular achievement in a field; one common definition of it is as a "period when a specified art, skill, or activity is at its peak." The term, though, is commonly used in a retrospective fashion, looking back with nostalgia at a better time, regardless if that was really the case. Its use, then is often flavored with a tinge of regret of having missed out on an era of epic accomplishment.

It's difficult to know when you're in the midst of a golden age, and perhaps a bit hubristic to declare one exists while it's still ongoing. Nonetheless, one can make a strong case that we're in some kind of golden age today for the search for and study of extrasolar planets, or exoplanets. Two decades ago the only confirmed exoplanets orbited a pulsar, and just how common planets were around stars more like our Sun was very much an open question. Today, confirmed exoplanets number in the hundreds, with thousands more waiting to be confirmed.

The vibrancy of this field of astronomy was evident at the 221st Meeting of the American Astronomical Society (AAS), held in Long Beach, California, last week. The meeting was full of sessions, plenary talks, and press conferences associated with exoplanet studies, from the latest discoveries of new planets to efforts to try and characterize the ones already found and also better understand how frequent such planets—particularly those like the Earth—are around other stars.

The wealth of findings at the conference caused even veteran exoplanet researchers to gush. "It's been an extraordinary AAS meeting already for those of you interested in exoplanets," said Geoff Marcy at beginning of a talk a day and a half into the four-day meeting. "The results that have been described by so many speakers already I think have been stunning, actually historic."

KEPLER'S BOUNTY

A major reason for that "stunning" perception has been NASA's Kepler mission. The spacecraft, launched nearly four years ago, has become an exoplanet discovery machine. Staring at the same spot in the sky, simultaneously observing more than 100,000 stars, Kepler is designed to detect minute, periodic decreases in brightness in these stars as exoplanets pass, or transit, across the disc of the star.

At last week's AAS meeting, scientists announced the discovery of 461 new "planet candidates," bringing the total of such discoveries by the spacecraft to 2,740. The number of these potential candidates that have been confirmed as exoplanets by other observations is much smaller: only 105 as of the AAS meeting. However, project scientists believe that most of these candidates are actual planets, since the false positive rate has typically been only 10%.

"We're learning as the years have gone by that the reliability of this catalog is quite high," said Natalie Batalha, Kepler mission scientist at NASA Ames Research Center, during a plenary talk at the conference. "It's likely that 90% or more of these are going to be bona fide planets." She then showed an updated chart of exoplanet discoveries, with the Kepler planet candidates dominating the display, triggering an impromptu round of applause from the audience.

"Kepler has transformed the field of exoplanet science," she continued. "There's probably not a single exoplanet scientist in the country who is not working right now on Kepler data."

Much of the media attention devoted to Kepler has been on individual exoplanet discoveries, including those that, at least in size and orbit, are increasingly like the Earth. One such discovery touted at the conference was a planet candidate designated KOI-172.02, a planet located in the habitable zone of a Sun-like star. That planet has an estimated radius 1.5 times of the Earth, so it is not exactly an Earth twin. "This is certainly more in the regime of the 'super-Earth' category," said Christopher Burke of the SETI Institute at a press conference about the Kepler discoveries.

Kepler's ultimate mission, though, is not one of individual exoplanet discoveries but of statistics. By looking at one small, representative sample of the sky, project scientists hope to gather information on the relative occurrence of exoplanet systems in general. And initial data confirms the expectations of many scientists: other solar systems are commonplace. One study used Kepler data to estimate that one sixth of Sun-like stars have an Earth-sized planet close in, with a period of 85 days or less.

Francois Fressin of the Harvard-Smithsonian Center for Astrophysics (CfA) noted that there are even slightly higher occurrences of super-Earths and Neptune-sized planets in those close orbits. Taking those planets into account, and extrapolating for longer orbital periods, he estimated than 70 to 90 percent of stars have planetary systems. "Almost all Sun-like stars have a planetary system," he said.

What remains to be determined, though, is what scientists call "eta-Earth": the frequency of stars with planets like the Earth in both size and orbit. Determining eta-Earth remains a primary goal of the Kepler mission, but project scientists said they need more data to make that determination. "It behooves us to continue observing for another four years to get a robust statistic on the frequency of Earth-sized planets," Batalha said.

Kepler, having completed its prime 3.5-year mission, is now in an extended mission that scientists hope will go long enough to collect enough data to make that eta-Earth calculation possible. "The Kepler spacecraft is operating very well," Kepler project scientist Steve Howell told a town hall meeting about the mission during the AAS conference. The main concern about the spacecraft's long-term health is regarding its reaction wheels, after one failed last year. "We are now operating on three reaction wheels. The Kepler spacecraft is doing fine on three wheels," he said.

M-CLASS PLANETS AROUND M-CLASS STARS

Although the focus of exoplanet searches has primarily been with Sun-like stars, a new theme emerged from the AAS conference: a new emphasis on smaller M-class red dwarf stars. These stars, it turns out, might hold the best chance for finding an Earth-like world—which Star Trek fans will recall, coincidentally, were designated M-class worlds in the original series—in the near future.

Studying M-class stars offer several advantages for exoplanet researchers. One is the sheer number of such stars: about 75 percent of the stars in the galaxy are M dwarfs. "You can think of them as the galaxy's silent majority," said John Johnson, a Caltech professor, in a plenary talk. "We're rare," he said of our own solar system, "simply because we don't orbit an M dwarf. And I think that's really profound."

At a separate meeting of NASA's Exoplanet Exploration Program Analysis Group, or ExoPAG, held in Long Beach immediately before the AAS meeting, David Charbonneau of the CfA noted that looking for terrestrial planets in habitable zones around M-class stars is considerably easier that for larger stars. Such planets offer deeper and more frequent transits because of their larger size relative to the star and closer orbits.

Charbonneau's group is seeking to look for such planets with a project called MEarth, using small robotic telescopes to look for transits by Earth-sized planets around such stars. That project has discovered only one such planet over its first four years, designated GJ 1214b. "It's kind of a run of the mill planet" other than that it orbits a red dwarf, said Zachory K. Berta of Harvard in an AAS conference presentation. That discovery rate is in line with the frequency of such planets MEarth could detect, based on Kepler data, he added; changes in observing strategy should increase the discovery rate by a factor of two to four.

Another Harvard student, Courtney Dressing, stated at the meeting that, based on existing data, there should be 0.06 planets in the habitable zone per small star. That means there is, with 95% confidence, an Earth-like planet within 31 parsecs of our Sun.

"If it so happens that M dwarfs make habitable zone planets," Charbonneau said at the ExoPAG meeting, "then it's a lock that the closest habitable zone planet to us, the closest habitable planet to us, orbits an M dwarf."

EXOCOMETS, EXOMOONS, AND OTHER EXOTICA

Our solar system, though, is more than just planets: there are dozens of moons and many more asteroids and comets. These would seem to be too small to be seen around other stars from the Earth, but astronomers at the meeting reported evidence for at least some of these smaller bodies.

Barry Welch of the University of California Berkeley announced the discovery of several "exocomet" systems, based on distinctive spectral lines seen around young stars. This is, he described at a press conference, further evidence of the formation of solar systems. "We've found essentially the leftover building blocks of planetary systems," he said.

Others reported evidence of "exoasteroids" by detecting so-called "polluted" white dwarfs, whose spectra contain the signatures of asteroidal material that have accreted onto the stars. "I think the conclusion you can draw," said John Debes of the Space Telescope Science Institute about his and others' research, "is that there are a lot of asteroids everywhere."

Debes and others ruled out alternative sources for the white dwarf pollution, such as the interstellar medium. Ben Zuckerman of UCLA, who reported on the discovery of a planetary system in the Hyades star cluster by detecting calcium lines in the star's spectra, argued that discovery likely means planets are also orbiting it. "You wouldn't expect asteroids orbiting around a white dwarf to just be changing their orbits and falling onto their star unless something was perturbing their orbits significantly," he said. "You really need those planets to change the orbits."

Other studies of these planetesimals suggest they're like the material that made the Earth. "To zero order, extrasolar minor planets resemble Earth" in terms of their composition, said Michael Jura of UCLA in a plenary talk. "We have yet to discover anything truly exotic or completely unfamiliar."

Exomoons, though, still remain beyond the grasp of scientists, at least for now. David Kipping of Harvard reported on the first results of the Hunt for Exomoons with Kepler effort, looking at a very tiny sample—seven—of planet candidates from the Kepler catalog. None of those seven showed any signs of moons, although he noted in four cases they were able to set an upper limit on the size of any moon of 4% of the mass of the planet.

FUTURE PLANS

As the numbers of exoplanets grow, scientists are increasingly interested to try and learn more about them than just basic characteristics like mass, radius, and orbit. That pushes the limits of what's possible today with ground- and space-based telescopes.

"The key diagnostic technique [in astronomy] is spectroscopy," said Marcy at the ExoPAG meeting. That, however, is difficult for most exoplanets. "To allow the exoplanet field to mature into a domain similar to the rest of astrophysics, we have to be able to take spectra."

There has been some spectroscopy done of exoplanets, particularly of "hot Jupiters," gas giants closely orbiting their parent stars. That has enabled some knowledge of their atmosphere, including composition, temperature profiles, and winds, Heather Knutson of Caltech explained in a plenary talk at the meeting. "We have a lot of theories, we've got some interesting patterns, but we're still trying to figure out how to fit the two together," she said.

Studying more exoplanets, particularly smaller ones, may require new telescopes. At the ExoPAG meeting, Marcy argued for an exoplanet mission using one of the two 2.4-meter telescopes "donated" to NASA last year by the National Reconnaissance Office. "I think there's a great opportunity to do spectroscopy of Jupiters and Neptunes around the nearest stars" with such an observatory, he said.

Immediately before the ExoPAG meeting, NASA announced it was chartering two science and technology definition teams to study concepts for exoplanet direct imaging missions. One will examine the use of an internal coronagraph to block light from the star to enable direct detection, while the other will study use of external starshades to accomplish the same thing. The goal will be to develop "probe-class" mission concepts with a total cost of $1 billion; those studies will be completed by early 2015 to support NASA planning for future missions later in the decade, after the completion of the James Webb Space Telescope (JWST).

Without a firm commitment to a dedicated exoplanet mission—and concerns about the funding for astrophysics missions in general later in the decade at NASA, given uncertainty about the agency's long-term budget—some astronomers worry that the pace of exoplanet research could stumble, particularly when

Kepler's mission ends in several years. Another space-craft that detected exoplanets by means of observing transits, France's CoRoT spacecraft, suffered a malfunction in orbit last year and many fear the spacecraft is lost.

Others, though, are more optimistic about the future, seeing opportunities to continue exoplanet studies with ground-based telescopes and JWST and, later, the Wide-Field Infrared Survey Telescope (WFIRST) space telescope. It's possible, then, that despite all the excitement about exoplanet research present at the AAS meeting, the real golden age of exoplanet studies, including finding true Earth-like worlds, may still be yet to come.

1. How much do we know about planets suitable for human life beyond our solar system?

2. What kinds of planets, according to the most recent research, would be most suitable for space colonization, and why?

CHAPTER 5

WHAT ORDINARY PEOPLE SAY

While everybody is entitled to their own opinion, there are certain topics that require quite a bit of knowledge for an opinion to have any merit. Space travel is certainly among those more specialized topics, as the challenges it presents are far removed from the daily life of the average citizen—at least for now. Space tourism may still be reserved for the very rich, and trips to other planets may still be a long way off, but as experts continue their efforts, the chance increases that it will have an impact on ordinary people.

Today, it is unknown whether going to space will be an affordable option for a larger number of people any time soon (or even at all). But even if the benefits are not as direct, research conducted in the pursuit of space exploration has developed numerous technologies—from artificial limbs to improved solar cells—that have improved life on Earth. Even though it might not be possible for everybody to travel to Mars, it will still affect everybody if just one person is able to make the trip.

"THE HIGH FRONTIER, REDUX," BY CHARLES STROSS, JUNE 16, 2007

I write SF [science fiction] for a living. Possibly because of this, folks seem to think I ought to be an enthusiastic proponent of space exploration and space colonization. Space exploration? Yep, that's a fair cop — I'm all in favour of advancing the scientific enterprise. But actual space *colonisation* is another matter entirely, and those of a sensitive (or optimistic) disposition might want to stop reading right now ...

I'm going to take it as read that the *idea* of space colonization isn't unfamiliar; domed cities on Mars, orbiting cylindrical space habitats a la J. D. Bernal or Gerard K. O'Neill, that sort of thing. Generation ships that take hundreds of years to ferry colonists out to other star systems where — as we are now discovering — there are profusions of planets to explore.

And I don't want to spend much time talking about the unspoken ideological underpinnings of the urge to space colonization, other than to point out that they're *there*, that the case for space colonization isn't usually presented as an economic enterprise so much as a quasi-religious one. "We can't afford to keep all our eggs in one basket" isn't so much a justification as an appeal to sentimentality, for in the hypothetical case of a planet-trashing catastrophe, we (who currently inhabit the surface of the Earth) are dead anyway. The *future* extinction of the human species cannot affect you if you are already dead: strictly speaking, it should be of no personal concern.

Historically, crossing oceans and setting up farmsteads on new lands conveniently stripped of indigenous inhabitants by disease has been a cost-effective proposition. But the scale factor involved in space travel is strongly counter-intuitive.

Here's a handy metaphor: let's approximate one astronomical unit — the distance between the Earth and the sun, roughly 150 million kilometres, or 600 times the distance from the Earth to the Moon — to *one centimetre*. Got that? 1AU = 1cm. (You may want to get hold of a ruler to follow through with this one.)

The solar system is conveniently small. Neptune, the outermost planet in our solar system, orbits the sun at a distance of almost exactly 30AU, or 30 centimetres — one foot (in imperial units). Giant Jupiter is 5.46 AU out from the sun, almost exactly two inches (in old money).

We've sent space probes to Jupiter; they take two and a half years to get there if we send them on a straight Hohmann transfer orbit, but we can get there a bit faster using some fancy orbital mechanics. Neptune is still a stretch — only one spacecraft, Voyager 2, has made it out there so far. Its journey time was 12 years, and it wasn't stopping. (It's now on its way out into interstellar space, having passed the heliopause some years ago.)

The Kuiper belt, domain of icy wandering dwarf planets like Pluto and Eris, extends perhaps another 30AU, before merging into the much more tenuous Hills cloud and Oort cloud, domain of loosely coupled long-period comets.

Now for the first scale shock: using our handy metaphor the Kuiper belt is perhaps a metre in diameter. The Oort cloud, in contrast, is as much as 50,000 AU in radius — its outer edge lies *half a kilometre* away.

Got that? Our planetary solar system is 30 centimetres, roughly a foot, in radius. But to get to the edge of the Oort cloud, you have to go half a kilometre, roughly a third of a mile.

Next on our tour is Proxima Centauri, our nearest star. (There might be a brown dwarf or two lurking unseen in the icy depths beyond the Oort cloud, but if we've spotted one, I'm unaware of it.) Proxima Centauri is 4.22 light years away. A light year is 63.2×10^3 AU, or 9.46×10^{12} Km. So Proxima Centauri, at 267,000 AU, is just under two and a third kilometres, or two miles (in old money) away from us.

But Proxima Centauri is a poor choice, if we're looking for habitable real estate. While exoplanets are apparently common as muck, *terrestrial* planets are harder to find; Gliese 581c, the first such to be detected (and it looks like a pretty weird one, at that), is roughly 20.4 light years away, or using our metaphor, about ten miles.

Try to get a handle on this: it takes us 2-5 years to travel two inches. But the proponents of interstellar travel are talking about journeys of *ten miles*. That's the first point I want to get across: that if the distances involved in interplanetary travel are enormous, and the travel times fit to rival the first Australian settlers, then the distances and times involved in *interstellar* travel are mind-numbing.

This is not to say that interstellar travel is impossible; quite the contrary. But to do so effectively you need either (a) outrageous amounts of cheap energy, or (b) highly efficient robot probes, or (c) a magic wand. And in the absence of (c) you're not going to get any news back from the other end in less than decades. Even if (a) is achievable, or by means of (b) we can send self-replicating factories and have them turn distant solar systems into hives of industry, and more speculatively find some way to transmit human beings there, they are going to have zero net economic impact on *our* circumstances (except insofar as sending them out costs us money).

What do I mean by outrageous amounts of cheap energy?

Let's postulate that in the future, it will be possible to wave a magic wand and construct a camping kit that encapsulates all the necessary technologies and information to rebuild a human civilization capable of eventually sending out interstellar colonization missions — a bunch of self-replicating, self-repairing robotic hardware, and a downloadable copy of the sum total of human knowledge to date. Let's *also* be generous and throw in a closed-circuit life support system capable of keeping a human occupant alive indefinitely, for many years at a stretch, with zero failures and losses, and capable where necessary of providing medical intervention. Let's throw in a willing astronaut (the fool!) and stick them inside this assembly. It's going to be pretty boring in there, but I think we can conceive of our minimal manned interstellar mission as being about the size and mass of a Mercury capsule. And I'm going to nail a target to the barn door and call it 2000kg in total.

(Of course we can cut corners, but I've already invoked self-replicating robotic factories and closed-cycle life support systems, and those are close enough to magic wands as it is. I'm going to deliberately *ignore* more speculative technologies such as starwisps, mind transfer, or AIs sufficiently powerful to operate autonomously — although I used them shamelessly in my novel Accelerando. What I'm trying to do here is come up with a useful metaphor for the energy budget realistically required for interstellar flight.)

Incidentally, a probe massing 1-2 tons with an astronaut on top is a bit implausible, but a 1-2 ton probe could conceivably carry enough robotic instrumentation to do useful research, plus a laser powerful enough to punch a signal home, and maybe even that shrink-wrapped military/industrial complex in a tin can that would allow it to build something useful at the other end. Anything much smaller, though, isn't going to be able to transmit its findings to us — at least, not without some breakthroughs in communication technology that haven't shown up so far.

Now, let's say we want to deliver our canned monkey to Proxima Centauri within its own lifetime. We're sending them on a one-way trip, so a 42 year flight time isn't unreasonable. (Their job is to supervise the machinery as it unpacks itself and begins to brew up a bunch of new colonists using an artificial uterus. Okay?) This means they need to achieve a mean cruise speed of 10% of the speed of light. They then need to decelerate at the other end. At 10% of c relativistic effects are minor — there's going to be time dilation, but it'll be on the order of hours or days over the duration of the 42-year voyage. So we need to accelerate our astronaut to 30,000,000 metres per second, and decelerate them at the other end. Cheating and using Newton's laws of motion, the kinetic energy acquired by acceleration is 9×10^{17} Joules, so we can call it 2×10^{18} Joules in round numbers for the entire trip. NB: This assumes that the propulsion system in use is 100% efficient at converting energy into momentum, that there are no losses from friction with the interstellar medium, and that the propulsion source is external — that is, there's no need to take reaction mass along en route. So this is a *lower bound* on the energy cost of transporting our Mercury-capsule sized expedition to Proxima Centauri in less than a lifetime.

To put this figure in perspective, the total conversion of one kilogram of mass into energy yields 9×10^{16} Joules. (Which one of my sources informs me, is about equivalent to 21.6 megatons in thermonuclear explosive yield). So we require the equivalent energy output to 400 megatons of nuclear armageddon in order to move a capsule of about the gross weight of a fully loaded Volvo V70 automobile to Proxima Centauri in less than a human lifetime. That's the same as the yield of the entire US Minuteman III ICBM force.

For a less explosive reference point, our entire planetary economy runs on roughly 4 terawatts of electricity (4×10^{12} watts). So it would take our total planetary electricity production for a period of half a million seconds — roughly 5 days — to supply the necessary va-va-voom.

But to bring this back to earth with a bump, let me just remind you that this probe is so implausibly efficient that it's veering back into "magic wand" territory. I've tap-danced past a 100% efficient power transmission system capable of operating across interstellar distances with pinpoint precision and no conversion losses, and that allows the spacecraft on the receiving end to convert power directly into momentum. This is not exactly like any power transmission system that anyone's built to this date, and I'm not sure I can see where it's coming from.

Our one astronaut, 10% of c mission approximates well to an unmanned flight, but what about longer-term expeditions? Generation ships are a staple of SF; they're slow (probably under 1% of c) and they carry a self-sufficient city-state. The crew who set off won't live to see their destination (the flight time to Proxima Centauri at 1% of c is about 420 years), but the vague hope is that *someone* will. Leaving aside our lack of a proven track record at building social institutions that are stable across time periods greatly in excess of a human lifespan, using a generation ship probably doesn't do much for our energy budget problem either. A society of human beings are likely to need more space and raw material to do stuff with while in flight; sticking a solitary explorer in a tin can for forty-something years is merely cruel and unusual, but doing it to an entire city for several centuries probably qualifies as a crime against humanity. We therefore need to relax the mass constraint. Assuming the same super-efficient life support as our solitary explorer, we might postulate that each colonist requires ten tons of structural mass to move around in. (About the same as a large trailer home. For *life*.) We've cut the peak velocity by an order of magnitude, but we've increased the payload requirement by an order of magnitude *per passenger* — and we need enough passengers to make a stable society fly. I'd guess a sensible lower number would be on the order of 200 people, the size of a prehistoric primate troupe. (Genetic diversity? I'm going to assume we can hand-wave around that by packing some deep-frozen sperm and ova, or frozen embryos, for later reuse.) By the time we work up to a minimal generation ship (and how minimal can we get, confining 200 human beings in an object weighing aout 2000 tons, for roughly the same period of time that has elapsed since the Plymouth colony landed in what was later to become Massachusetts [sic]?) we're actually requiring much *more* energy than our solitary high-speed explorer.

And remember, this is only what it takes to go to *Proxima Centauri* our *nearest* neighbour. Gliese 581c is five times as far away. Planets that are *already* habitable insofar as they orbit inside the habitable zone of their star, possess free oxygen in their atmosphere, and have a mass, surface gravity and escape velocity that are not too forbidding, are likely to be somewhat rarer. (And if there is free oxygen in the atmosphere on a planet, that implies something else — the presence of pre-existing photosynthetic life, a carbon cycle, and a bunch of other stuff that could well unleash a big can of whoop-ass on an unprimed human immune system. The question of how we might interact with alien biologies is an order of magnitude bigger and more complex than the question of how we might get there — and the preliminary outlook is rather forbidding.)

The long and the short of what I'm trying to get across is quite simply that, in the absence of technology indistinguishable from magic — magic tech that, furthermore, does things that from today's perspective appear to play fast and loose with the laws of physics — interstellar travel for human beings is near-as-dammit a non-starter.

And while I won't rule out the possibility of such seemingly-magical technology appearing at some time in the future, the conclusion I draw *as a science fiction writer* is that if interstellar colonization ever happens, it will *not* follow the pattern of historical colonization drives that are followed by mass emigration and trade between the colonies and the old home soil.

What about our own solar system?

After contemplating the vastness of interstellar space, our own solar system looks almost comfortingly accessible at first. *Exploring* our own solar system is a no-brainer: we can do it, we *are* doing it, and interplanetary exploration is probably going to be seen as one of the great scientific undertakings of the late 20th and early 21st century, when the history books get written.

But when we start examining the prospects for interplanetary *colonization* things turn gloomy again.

Bluntly, we're *not* going to get there by rocket ship.

Optimistic projects suggest that it should be possible, with the low cost rockets currently under development, to maintain a Lunar presence for a transportation cost of roughly $15,000 per kilogram. Some extreme projections suggest that if the cost can be cut to roughly triple the cost of fuel and oxidizer (meaning, the spacecraft concerned will be both largely reusable and *very cheap*) then we might even get as low as $165/kilogram to the lunar surface. At *that* price, sending a 100Kg astronaut to Moon Base One looks as if it ought to cost not much more than a first-class return air fare from the UK to New Zealand ... except that such a price estimate is hogwash. We primates have certain failure modes, and one of them that must not be underestimated is our tendency to irreversibly malfunction when exposed to climactic extremes of temperature, pressure, and partial pressure of oxygen. While the amount of oxygen, water, and food a human consumes per day doesn't sound all that serious — it probably totals roughly ten kilograms, if you economize and recycle the washing-up water — the amount of parasitic weight you need to keep the monkey from blowing out is measured in tons. A Russian Orlan-M space suit (which, some would say, is better than anything NASA has come up with over the years — take heed of the pre-breathe time requirements!) weighs 112 kilograms, which pretty much puts a floor on our infrastructure requirements. An actual habitat would need to mass a whole lot more. Even at $165/kilogram, that's going to add up to a very hefty excess baggage charge on that notional first class air fare to New Zealand — and I think the $165/kg figure is in any case highly unrealistic; even the authors of the article I cited thought $2000/kg was a bit more reasonable.

Whichever way you cut it, sending a single tourist to the moon is going to cost not less than $50,000 — and a more realistic figure, for a mature reusable, cheap, rocket-based lunar transport cycle is more like $1M. And that's before you factor in the price of bringing them back ...

The moon is about 1.3 light seconds away. If we want to go panning the (metaphorical) rivers for gold, we'd do better to send teleoperator-controlled robots; it's close enough that we can control them directly, and far enough away that the cost of transporting food and creature comforts for human explorers is astronomical. There probably *are* niches for human workers on a moon base, but only until our robot technologies are somewhat more mature than they are today; Mission Control would be a lot happier with a pair of hands and a high-def camera that doesn't talk back and doesn't need to go to the toilet or take naps.

When we look at the rest of the solar system, the picture is even bleaker. Mars is ... well, the phrase "tourist resort" springs to mind, and is promptly filed in the same corner as "Gobi desert". As Bruce Sterling has puts it [sic]: "I'll believe in people settling Mars at about the same time I see people settling the Gobi Desert. The Gobi Desert is about a thousand times as hospitable as Mars and five hundred times cheaper and easier to reach. Nobody ever writes "Gobi Desert Opera" because, well, it's just kind of plonkingly obvious that there's no good reason to go there and live. It's ugly, it's inhospitable and there's no way to make it pay. Mars is just the same, really. We just romanticize it because it's so hard to reach." In other words, going there to *explore* is fine and dandy — our robots are all over it already. But as a desirable residential neighbourhood it has some shortcomings, starting with the slight lack of breathable air and the sub-Antarctic nighttime temperatures and the Mach 0.5 dust storms, and working down from there.

Actually, there probably *is* a good reason for sending human explorers to Mars. And that's the distance: at up to 30 minutes, the speed of light delay means that remote control of robots on the Martian surface is extremely tedious. Either we need autonomous robots that can be assigned tasks and carry them out without direct human supervision, or we need astronauts in orbit or on the ground to boss the robot work gangs around.

On the other hand, Mars is a good way further away than the moon, and has a deeper gravity well. All of which drive up the cost per kilogram delivered to the Martian surface. Maybe FedEx could cut it as low as $20,000 per kilogram, but I'm not holding my breath.

Let me repeat myself: we are not going there with rockets. At least, not the conventional kind — and while there may be a role for nuclear propulsion in deep space, in general there's a trade-off between instantaneous thrust and efficiency; the more efficient your motor, the lower the actual thrust it provides. Some technologies such as the variable specific impulse magnetoplasma rocket show a good degree of flexibility, but in general they're not suitable for getting us from Earth's surface into orbit — they're only useful for trucking things around from low earth orbit on out.

Again, as with interstellar colonization, there are other options. Space elevators, if we build them, will invalidate a lot of what I just said. Some analyses of the energy costs of space elevators suggest that a marginal cost of $350/kilogram to geosynchronous orbit should be achievable without waving any magic wands (other than the enormous practical materials and structural engineering problems of building the thing in the first place). So we probably *can* look forward to zero-gee vacations in orbit, at a price. And space elevators are attractive because they're a scalable technology; you can use one to haul into space the material to build more. So, long term, space elevators *may* give us not-unreasonably priced access to space, including jaunts to the lunar surface for a price equivalent to less than $100,000 in today's money. At which point, settlement would begin to look economically feasible, except ...

We're human beings. We evolved to flourish in a very specific environment that covers perhaps 10%

of our home planet's surface area. (Earth is 70% ocean, and while we can survive, with assistance, in extremely inhospitable terrain, be it arctic or desert or mountain, we aren't well-adapted to thriving there.) Space itself is a very poor environment for humans to live in. A simple pressure failure can kill a spaceship crew in minutes. And that's not the only threat. Cosmic radiation poses a serious risk to long duration interplanetary missions, and unlike solar radiation and radiation from coronal mass ejections the energies of the particles responsible make shielding astronauts extremely difficult. And finally, there's the travel time. Two and a half years to Jupiter system; six months to Mars [sic].

Now, these problems are subject to a variety of approaches — including medical ones: does it matter if cosmic radiation causes long-term cumulative radiation exposure leading to cancers if we have advanced side-effect-free cancer treatments? Better still, if hydrogen sulphide-induced hibernation turns out to be a practical technique in human beings, we may be able to sleep through the trip. But even so, when you get down to it, there's not really any economically viable activity on the horizon for people to engage in that would require them to settle on a planet or asteroid and live there for the rest of their lives. In general, when we need to extract resources from a hostile environment we tend to build infrastructure to exploit them (such as oil platforms) but we don't exactly scurry to move our families there. Rather, crews go out to work a long shift, then return home to take their leave. After all, there's no *there* there — just a howling wilderness of north Atlantic gales and frigid water that will kill you within five minutes of exposure. And that, I submit, is the closest metaphor we'll find for interplanetary colonization. Most of the heavy lifting more than a million kilometres from Earth will be done by robots, overseen by human supervisors who will be itching to get home and spend their hardship pay. And closer to home, the commercialization of space will be incremental and slow, driven by our increasing dependence on near-earth space for communications, positioning, weather forecasting, and (still in its embryonic stages) tourism. But the domed city on Mars is going to have to wait for a magic wand or two to do something about the climate, or reinvent a kind of human being who can thrive in an airless, inhospitable environment.

Colonize the Gobi desert, colonize the North Atlantic in winter — *then* get back to me about the rest of the solar system!

1. What do you think about this popular science fiction writer's take on colonizing outer space? Is it disheartening to read such a cynical perspective on our current ability to reach other planets or stars from such an author?

2. Do you think the incredible interstellar distances make space colonization impossible?

"AMERICANS KEEN ON SPACE EXPLORATION, LESS SO ON PAYING FOR IT," FROM THE PEW RESEARCH CENTER, APRIL 23, 2014

Many Americans are optimistic about the future of space travel, but they don't necessarily want to pay for it.

It's been that way for some time, actually. A Harris survey taken in 1970 – less than a year after the first moon landing – showed that a majority (56%) thought the landing was not worth the money spent. A separate Harris poll, in 1971, however, found that 81% of Americans agreed with the statement that "nothing can equal seeing the astronauts land and walk on the moon as it happened live on TV."

In fact, as we dug through data archives of the National Opinion Research Center's General Social Survey — which has been asking the public for 40 years about their views of space exploration and federal funding for it — we found that Americans are consistently more likely to say that the U.S. spends too much on space exploration than too little. At no time has more than 22% of the public said that the U.S. spends too little on space exploration.

Still, that doesn't mean Americans aren't optimistic about exploring the possibilities of space. In a Pew Research Center/Smithsonian magazine survey released last week, a third of Americans said they believe there will be manned long-term colonies on other planets by the year 2064, despite evidence suggesting the difficulties of accomplishing that. Also, 63% of respondents to our 2010 survey said that they believe astronauts will have landed on Mars by 2050. More than half said that ordinary humans will be able to participate in space travel.

And it's not as though Americans have a dim view of NASA, which overseas the government's space program. About three quarters of Americans view NASA favorably – second only to the Centers for Disease Control and Prevention among federal agencies – according to a 2013 Pew Research survey.

Despite these positive opinions of the space program, just a two-in-ten Americans in the 2012 GSS survey said that the U.S. spends too little on space exploration. Four-in-ten believed the current spending was adequate, while three-in-ten believed further cuts should be made to the program. Instead, Americans strongly preferred increased spending on programs closer to home, including education (76%), public health (59%), and developing alternative energy sources (59%).

Currently, total funding for NASA accounts for 0.5% of the federal government's budget. Of that funding, the space exploration program accounts for roughly 22% of NASA's budget.

The disinclination to spend money on space exploration has already had an impact when it comes to ambitious projects like space colonization. In 2012, the NASA budget took a 20% hit to its planetary science programs, severely crippling NASA's Mars exploration program. This year, the budget for Opportunity, NASA's decade-old Mars rover, may be eliminated.

1. If funding is being cut to NASA, do you think NASA's plan for Mars colonization is still a reasonable goal?

2. Do you think the disinclination many Americans have to spend more federal money on space exploration will make it easier for private companies, like Mars One, to send the first human colonists to space?

"MARS HOPEFULS PONDER LIFE WITHOUT FAMILIES, FAVORITE FOODS," BY ELIZABETH LANDAU, FROM CNN, MAY 16, 2014

If your romantic partner pointed you to an application for a one-way trip to Mars, would you be upset -- or thrilled?

When Dr. Leila Zucker's husband sent her such an e-mail last spring, he said that he didn't want her to go but that he'd be a lousy husband if he didn't tell her about it.

Fast-forward to today: Zucker has made it past the first round of cuts for Mars One, a nonprofit organization that aims to send four people to the Red Planet in 2024 and subsequent groups in later years.

"Most of us want to explore, want to go new places, and then it's just a question of: How much are you willing to give up to do it?" she said.

Zucker is one of 705 candidates selected from a pool of 200,000 applicants for the mission. The select group has been narrowed from 1,058 people as some prospective astronauts dropped out for personal or medical reasons, Mars One said recently.

All of the remaining candidates will be interviewed by the Mars One selection committee.

Eventually, only four will be picked for the first trip. Apparently, none of them is scared off by the idea that, because of technological and financial limitations, Mars One astronauts would probably never come home.

IT MIGHT NOT ACTUALLY HAPPEN

Despite growing excitement surrounding this effort, it is not clear that sufficient money will be raised to follow through. Mars One CEO Bas Lansdorp has said the company is looking at "a range of funding scenarios."

A reality TV concept is one way Mars One may make good on its $6 billion budget for getting the first four humans to Mars. Lansdorp hopes the unprecedented video opportunities will attract sponsors, partners and media coverage.

But since no one has ever been to Mars, the technology to fly people there and keep them alive has not been tested there, either. Lansdorp said last year that "no new inventions are needed to land humans on Mars," and the website says the "plan is built upon existing technologies available from proven suppliers." But the company will need to show that key systems involved in transportation and life support will work in untraversed territories.

Mars One announced in March that it will soon begin constructing the first of its "simulation outposts" to train selected astronauts and teams, giving them experience in an environment made to feel like a Martian home.

Zucker, 46, an emergency medicine physician in Washington, is doubtful that Mars One will deliver on the trip at all. But if it does happen, she is on board. "There's no question."

SETTLING AWAY FROM YOUR SPOUSE

You might think that trying to emigrate from our planet might put some pressure on Earth-based relationships.

Zucker and her husband have been married for 21 years and have no children. If she goes to Mars, she said, she will probably offer her husband a divorce but will wear her wedding ring regardless. He doesn't want her to go, she said, but supports her following her dreams.

"Both of us are space enthusiasts," she said. "Humanity needs to expand off Earth if we expect the human race to succeed in any way beyond just basic survival."

Dan Carey, 52, another candidate, also believes humans should be spreading to other planets -- but his wife is not happy about Carey taking part in the mission. The couple, married 28 years, has two college-age children.

"She's concerned that she's going to have to watch me die on television," Carey said of his wife.

It's hard for Carey to think about leaving his wife and kids behind forever and never meeting future grandchildren. Still, he likes the idea of making history and seeing things that no one has seen directly before.

Sachin Desai and his wife, Ankita Ritwik, are getting around the marital tension issue by applying together. Desai says he could not go to Mars without her. Sure, Mars might challenge their marriage, but enough marriages are strained on Earth already, he said.

"One thing we do really well together is travel, and this would be a trip lasting the rest of our lives. I think we also are very good at helping each other out when we are stressed; I would be a far worse space cadet without her."

A 'SOCIAL EXPERIMENT'

When you live far from people you've known for a long time, you manage to make friends in your immediate area, and that's what Marina Santiago thinks will happen on Mars. The Harvard University Ph.D. student says Mars One crew members may take the place of friends, family and significant others.

Even if Mars One doesn't land people on Mars in 2025, it serves as a "social experiment" to get people talking and thinking about a Mars mission, she said.

"What I learned in grad school is that you never really know what problems you're going to come across until you actually try and do something. And the fact that they're actually trying to plan it, means that they'll come across the problems," she said. "I believe that there are no problems humanity can't solve."

Some candidates draw analogies to the early waves of European settlers in North America. Immigrants didn't have a rover on Plymouth Rock telling them about local conditions before they arrived, says Gregory Sachs.

"You even couldn't necessarily send a letter back to your family," Zucker said. "You were leaving everything for good. We at least will have the ability to use e-mail."

Still, it's a hard sell for friends of Brian Robles', a Mars One candidate who studies public health at Rutgers University.

"Usually, every time I tell somebody about the trip, they say it's a 'suicide mission' and 'you're going to die on

Mars,' " Robles said. "Well, we're going to die here, too. So might as well live your whole life to the fullest."

Funny he should mention that: The United Arab Emirates' religious watchdog, the General Authority of Islamic Affairs & Endowments, recently issued a fatwa to warn Muslims against the mission because "the chances of dying are higher than living."

Mars One responded in a statement, asking the authority to cancel the fatwa. "The Fatwa prohibits Muslims from going to Mars, but not from applying to Mars One's mission or training for the mission. In the next ten years, Mars One is open to working with the GAIAE to assess the risk of the mission as the unmanned settlement is under construction," Mars One said.

Sachs is hopeful that his trip wouldn't actually be one-way. He believes it would be in the best interest of the mission to send the astronauts back: "Imagine only the cost and tax on resources to care with someone elderly on a Mars One colony," he said.

But the way that the mission is currently set up -- with no return plan -- he's still interested.

MAKING HAPPY MARTIAN MEALS

Spending the rest of your life on another planet might make a person miss certain Earthly conveniences like favorite foods.

Carey said he'd lose weight just to be able to take more chocolate with him, since there would be a limit of how much weight each person could contribute to the mission.

Michael McDonnell, another applicant, said he wants to make the first pizza on Mars. Zucker would miss hamburgers but has high hopes for being able to grow them herself, perhaps from cow stem cells using a technique demonstrated last year.

"The first hardest thing to give up would obviously be my husband," Zucker said. "The second hardest thing would be meat."

But for this opportunity, she would kiss them both goodbye.

1. What seems to be the motivation for those who volunteered for the Mars One expedition?

2. Would you volunteer to travel to Mars? Why or why not?

CONCLUSION

S ome experts question whether or not we will be able to colonize outer space, given our technology at present. However, NASA and privately funded organizations have implemented plans to do so, and they are well on their way. Many such strategies plan for crewed flights to Mars will be possible by 2050. Thus, the public should regard our increasing manned exploration into space as a very likely possibility—and begin to think about all of its implications.

Establishing new colonies in the past has been a costly and risky venture, and a permanent Martian colony will be no different. Once we are technologically capable of space colonization, there are many lessons that can be learned from our experiences colonizing on Earth. To avoid potentially harmful disruptions to the colony, there are many actions to be considered in addition to the technical planning. This includes the setting of clear, achievable, goals for the colonists.

One of the major long-term goals should be the establishment of a separate Martian nation. Working towards such a goal will be difficult, and will probably require the modification of much existing space-oriented legislation, but the very act of progress towards this goal will increase the colonists' sense of ownership and motivation. When this is achieved, we will have created not only a successful and bright future for life on Mars, but an example that will provide insight into our daily lives here on Earth.

There are those who have already shown that they would be willing to captain humankind's first explorations to Mars. One day, we will watch their courageous voyages.

BIBLIOGRAPHY

"Agreement Governing the Activities of States on the Moon and Other Celestial Bodies." United Nations, December 18, 1979. Retrieved January 8, 2016 (http://www.unoosa.org/pdf/publications/ST_SPACE_061Rev01E.pdf).

Cain, Fraser. "The Value of Space Exploration." *Universe Today*, April 11, 2008. Retrieved May 11, 2016 (http://www.universetoday.com/13600/the-value-of-space-exploration).

Crowl, Adam. "Interstellar Comparisons." Icarus Interstellar, October 1, 2014. Retrieved January 8, 2016 (http://www.icarusinterstellar.org/interstellar-comparisons/).

Foust, Jeff. "A Golden Age of Exoplanet Science." *The Space Review*, January 14, 2013. Retrieved January 8, 2016 (http://www.thespacereview.com/article/2219/1).

Jobes, Douglas O. and Alan B. Wasser. "Space Land Claim Recognition: *Leveraging the Inherent Value of Lunar Land for Billions in Private Sector Investment.*" The Space Settlement Institute, August 9, 2004. Retrieved January 8, 2016 (http://ww.space-settlement-institute.org/Articles/LCRbrief.pdf).

Landau, Elizabeth. "Mars Hopefuls Ponder Life Without Families, Favorite Foods." *CNN,* May 16, 2014. Retrieved January 19, 2016 (http://www.cnn.com/2014/05/16/tech/innovation/mars-one-candidates/).

Listner, Michael, and Christopher Newman. "Failure to Launch: the Technical, Ethical, and Legal Case Against Mars One." *The Space Review,* March 16, 2015. Retrieved March 14, 2016 (http://www.thespacereview.com/article/2712/1).

"NASA's Journey to Mars. Pioneering Next Steps in Space Exploration." NASA, October 2015. Retrieved January 8, 2016 (http://www.nasa.gov/sites/default/files/atoms/files/journey-to-mars-next-steps-20151008_508.pdf).

Obama, Barack. "Remarks by the President on Space Exploration in the 21st Century." The White House, Office of the Press Secretary, April 15, 2010. Retrieved January 8, 2016 (https://www.whitehouse.gov/the-press-office/remarks-president-space-exploration-21st-century).

O'Neill, Ian. "Aldrin: Mars Pioneers Should Not Return to Earth." *Universe Today*, October 23, 2008. Retrieved May 11, 2016 (http://www.universetoday.com/19962/aldrin-mars-pioneers-should-not-return-to-earth).

Stross, Charles. "The High Frontier, Redux." June 16, 2007. Retrieved January 8. 2016 (http://www.antipope.org/charlie/blog-static/2007/06/the_high_frontier_redux.html).

Taverny, Thomas D. "To Mars, or, Not to Mars?" *The Space Review*, August 19, 2013. Retrieved January 8, 2016 (http://www.the spacereview.com/article/2350/1).

"Treaty on Principles Governing the Activities of States in the Exploration and Use of Outer Space, including the Moon and Other Celestial Bodies." United Nations, January 27, 1967. Retrieved January 8, 2016 (http://www.unoosa.org/pdf/publications/ST_SPACE_061Rev01E.pdf).

Williams, Matt. "Will We Ever Colonize Mars?" *Universe Today*, May 31, 2015. Retrieved January 8, 2016 (http://www.universetoday.com/14883/mars-colonizing/).

Williams, Matt. "The Definitive Guide to Terraforming." *Universe Today*, February 23, 2016. Retrieved May 11, 2016 (http://www.universetoday.com/127311/guide-to-terraforming).

Wormald, Benjamin. "Americans Keen on Space Exploration, Less So on Paying For It." Pew Research Center, April 23, 2014. Retrieved May 11, 2016 (http://www.pewresearch.org/fact-tank/2014/04/23/americans-keen-on-space-exploration-less-so-on-paying-for-it/).

CHAPTER NOTES

CHAPTER 1: WHAT THE EXPERTS AND ACADEMICS SAY

"FAILURE TO LAUNCH: THE TECHNICAL, ETHICAL, AND LEGAL CASE AGAINST MARS ONE," BY MICHAEL LISTNER AND CHRISTOPHER NEWMAN

1. The Technology, Mars One Project, last visited March 9, 2015.
2. http://www.nasa.gov/home/hqnews/2012/mar/HQ_12-090_LAUNCH_Beyond_Waste.htm. See also http://www.paragonsdc.com.
3. Nancy Atkinson, "The Mars Landing Approach: Getting Large Payloads to the Surface of the Red Planet," July 17, 2007.
4. National Aeronautics and Space Administration, Supersonic Retropropulsion Technology Development in NASA's Entry, Descent, and Landing Project, Karl Edquist, Scott Berry, Bil Kleb, Ashley Korzun, Artem Dyakonov, Kerry Zarchi, Guy Schauerhamer, Ethan Post.
5. Sydney Do, Koki Ho, Samuel Schreiner, Andrew Owens, Olivier de Weck, AN INDEPENDENT ASSESSMENT OF THE TECHNICAL FEASIBILITY OF THE MARS ONE MISSION PLAN, 65th International Astronautical Congress, Toronto, Canada.
6. Elizabeth Howell, "Mars One Dustup: Founder Says Mission Won't Fail as MIT Study Predicts," October 14, 2014.
7. http://www.purduereview.com/science/the-early-failure-of-mars-one-and-why-it-matters/
8. http://www.bbc.co.uk/programmes/b03vpc74
9. Claude Lafleur, "Costs of US Piloted Programs," *The Space Review*, March 8, 2010
10. John Putman, "Mars One, the 'Third Quarter Effect,' and Our Human Journey into Deep Space," *The Space Review*, January 26, 2015.
11. Chris Chambers, "Mars One: The Psychology of Isolation, Confinement and 24-hour Big Brother," *The Guardian*, September 9, 2013.
12. Irene Klotz, "Mars Crew Guinea Pigs Suffered Insomnia, Lethargy," January 16, 2013.

13. "Will Psychological Issues Become a Problem for the Astronauts?," Mars One, last visited March 9, 2015.

14. Klotz, 2013.

15. James Kingland, "Bas Lansdorp Q&A: 'I Hope to Go to Mars Myself One Day,'" *The Guardian*, December 10, 2013.

16. U. S. v. The Nancy, 3 Wash. C. C. 287, Fed. Cas. No. 15,854.

17. Whether Mars One could successfully incorporate as a nonprofit organization in the United States is debatable. Nonprofit organizations in the United States are heavily scrutinized by the federal and state governments, and it's unclear whether the innocuous goals of Mars One could withstand the substantial regulatory scrutiny.

18. A common strawman argument from private space advocates is that jurisdiction under Article VI could be avoided if the private entity expatriates itself to a non-OST country such as Tonga and performs its activities from there. This approach is fundamentally flawed because even if the organization expatriates itself, Article VI could still reach to the individuals of the organization and follow them to the non-OST country. Beyond that, expatriation of a private entity to a non-OST country would also cut off resources vital to not only launch the precursor missions for Mars One, but also the high rate of supply and support needed not to mention further missions to grow the colony.

19. It's plausible that a launch license could be revoked; however, that would mean that the United States and the Netherlands, who both have continuing jurisdiction and responsibility over the Mars One and the colonists per Article VI of the OST, would be responsible for ensuring the colony survives, which means that resupply launches would have to be coordinated and paid for by the respective governments. Because of this possibility, Mars One would have to be under constant oversight and heavily scrutinized to ensure that it will not fail and meet its obligations to support the colony. This level of oversight will draw the ire of the purist approach to private space activities, but it is unavoidable.

GLOSSARY

AI—An acronym for Artifical Intelligence; machines or computer software capable of intelligent behavior that may one day play a role in human efforts of space exploration.

Apollo program—NASA's Apollo program from 1969 to 1972 was the first and so far only human spaceflight program that succeeded in bringing humans to the Moon.

ESA—The European Space Agency, an organization with twenty-two member states dedicated to space exploration.

exoplanet—A planet outside our solar system that orbits a star other than our Sun.

goldilocks zone—The habitable zone around a star where life is considered to be possible.

ISS—The International Space Station first launched in 1998, and is a human outpost in space used for scientific research.

JPL—The Jet Propulsion Laboratory, a NASA facility in La Cañada Flintridge, California, that focuses on constructing spacecraft.

Kepler—A space observatory named after astronomer Johannes Kepler and launched by NASA in 2009, which had discovered over one thousand exoplanets by 2015.

LEO—Low Earth Orbit, a region above Earth that extends up to 2000 km above sea level; the ISS is in Low Earth Orbit at about 250 miles (400 km) above sea level.

Mars One—A nonprofit organization founded in 2011 that has proposed a manned mission to Mars by 2027 followed by establishing a permanent colony.

NASA—The National Aeronautics and Space Administration, the American space agency established in 1958.

Orion—The Orion Multi-Purpose Crew Vehicle is a spacecraft under development by NASA to be launched on the SLS to reach destinations in Low Earth Orbit and beyond.

SLS — Space Launch System, a new launch system under development by NASA that is planned (among other missions) to be used for a crewed mission to Mars.

SpaceX — Space Exploration Technologies Corporation, an American company founded in 2002 by entrepreneur Elon Musk that pursues the goal of making the colonization of Mars possible.

FOR MORE INFORMATION

BOOKS

Aldrin, Buzz, and David Leonard. *Mission to Mars: My Vision for Space Exploration.* Washington, DC: National Geographic, 2013.

Aldrin, Buzz, and Marianne J. Dyson. *Welcome to Mars: Making a Home on the Red Planet.* Washington, DC: National Geographic, 2015.

Bignami, Giovanni F., and Andrea Sommariva. *A Scenario for Interstellar Exploration and Its Financing.* Milan, Italy: Springer, 2013.

Carroll, Michael W. *Living Among Giants: Exploring and Settling the Outer Solar System.* Cham, Switzerland: Springer, 2014.

Cockell, Charles, ed. *Human Governance Beyond Earth: Implications for Freedom.* Cham, Switzerland: Springer, 2015.

Lockard, Elizabeth Song. *Human Migration to Space: Alternative Technological Approaches for Long-Term Adaptation to Extraterrestrial Environments.* Cham, Switzerland: Springer, 2014.

Petranek, Stephen L. *How We'll Live on Mars.* New York: Simon & Schuster, 2015.

Smith, Cameron, M., and Evan T. Davies. *Emigrating Beyond Earth: Human Adaptation and Space Colonization.* New York: Springer, 2012.

WEBSITES

NASA: Space Settlements
settlement.arc.nasa.gov
> NASA's official website offers a plethora of information on space travel and research, including a collection of material on space settlements, starting with ideas developed at NASA in the 1970s.

The Mars Society
www.marssociety.org
> The Mars Society aims to further the exploration and settlement of Mars, and its website is a good resource for news on current developments regarding the Red Planet.

INDEX

ABOUT THE EDITOR

Dr. Nicki Peter Petrikowski is a literary scholar as well as an editor, author, and translator.

DATE DUE
